WISDOM IN
PRACTICE

Be ye wise as serpents and
harmless as doves

The present volume is one of a sequence of books by the same author on the application of the Ancient Wisdom to modern living:

THE FINDING OF THE THIRD EYE
THE INITIATION OF THE WORLD
THE FIFTH DIMENSION
WISDOM IN PRACTICE
THE SECRET OF THE ATOMIC AGE
WHEN HUMANITY COMES OF AGE
(Individual and World Fulfilment)

The author would be glad to hear from readers who are interested in the subject of human evolution and world progress. Letters may be sent to British Monomark/VSA, London WC1, or direct to the publisher who will forward them on to Miss Alder unopened.

WISDOM IN PRACTICE

Vera Stanley Alder

SAMUEL WEISER
New York
1972

First Published by Rider & Co.
This American Edition 1970
Second Impression 1972

S A M U E L W E I S E R , I N C .
734 Broadway
New York, N. Y. 10003

Printed in U.S.A. by
NOBLE OFFSET PRINTERS, INC.
New York, N.Y. 10003

Contents

Introduction   vii

Part I

SELF-ANALYSIS

1	To Begin With, What Are We?	3
2	Our Patriotism	16
3	Our Morality	23
4	Our Inhibitions	31
5	Our Double Natures	39
6	Are We Logical?	49
7	The Reckoning	58
8	Personal Armageddon	64
9	Rebirth	73

Part II

WORLD-ANALYSIS

10	Our World, What Is It?	79
11	World Morality	86
12	World Inhibitions	90
13	World Responsibility	94
14	World Armageddon	98
15	After Armageddon—What?	104

Part III

WISDOM IN PRACTICE

16 The New World   111
17 The Spiritual Laws   115
18 The Ten Commandments   126
19 'Thou Shalt Not . . .'   135
20 The Holy Ghost   143
21 World Faiths   149
22 Summing Up   155
23 Wisdom in Practice   164

THE AQUARIAN CHRISTIAN ASSOCIATION
A Non-Profit Effort, To Help People
To Help Each Other, Including Themselves
P. O. BOX 1813, SANTA FE, N.M. 87501

Introduction

When the United Nations was visioned and assembled there were evidently enough people of goodwill in the world to build an influence sufficiently strong to inspire our leaders to take that significant step forwards.

The concept of world unity and co-operation was at last publicly anchored on earth. Of course it was only a first step. There was much trial and error to be gone through which obviously still continues. The inaugurators tied their own hands by the form in which they allowed the veto to function. They had but little idea as to how to train or fuse the United Nations Forces which endeavoured to keep the peace. They could not design a successful form of sanctions or any equivalent. They could not even speak with one voice to compel disarmament, or, in fact, to uphold any of the Ten Commandments in any form in which they might interpret them.

The inspiration to unify was there. But the maturity wisely to understand how to take advantage of this great opportunity was completely missing. People everywhere were and are bogged down and stupefied by the world conditions inherited from the so-called Dark Ages. A world of 'grab' instead of 'give' has inevitably produced a growing accumulation of poisoning of all kinds —in air, water, soil, food, entertainment, education, industry and politics—the net result of greed, fear, opportunism and exploitation.

Not so long ago pioneer writers such as Tolstoy, Victor Hugo, Charles Dickens and many others, pointed out the evils which such attitudes created in social conditions. They did valiant work. But it took more than that to arouse the people to a recognition of the extent of their backwardness and underdevelopment. Even two world wars (really one continuous war not yet over) has only recently succeeded in impressing people with the dead-lock, the impasse into which humanity has forced itself through living without integrity, without allegiance to any spiritual prin-ciples whatever. This has caused the rot to go from bad to worse.

The eyes of the world, fixed from habit upon England, have witnessed first of all the crime wave (or flood!) then an invasion by the gambling world, quickly followed by the drug epidemic. Much of this was adopted by us from our 'offspring' the United States. Other countries seemed obliged to unload their unwanted or disinherited populace upon us. This was fair enough consider-ing that we had often done as we chose in those same countries. But all this came at a time when Great Britain was handicapped by labour difficulties and strikes, losing millions in the industrial world, so that people struggled on, taxed, redundant, confused and disheartened—until, finally, a new element arose in our midst, which at first seemed more violent and inconsequent than all the rest. It was the upsurge of rebellious youth—the young in revolt at last.

It gradually became obvious that this tide of revolt was world wide—taking much the same form at the same time in every land. Little by little, this form seemed to take a definite shape. The young people utterly despaired at the world in which they found themselves. Their elders seemed unwilling or incapable of sharing their awakening realisations and repulsions. They were thrown back upon each other, to discover at last that they were not alone, but that thousands of their age group had arrived at the same stage. In their violent repudiation of everything belong-ing to the way of life which they felt to be abhorrent, they first expressed rebellion through their way of living. If discipline, cleanliness, orthodox religion, education, clothing and customs had resulted in a world where the highest disease risk was suicide; where people lived under continual threat of horrible mass annihilation through the pressing of a button by some national power-gang with whom they had nothing to do; where so-called progress was causing poverty, homelessness, disease and misery; whilst world wealth and man-power was usurped in a prestige race to exploit other planets whilst leaving our own in a hopeless mess; where no remedy has been found for any of the major world problems, and where the last consideration is the development and fulfilment of man himself—then obviously some entirely new way of living with entirely new customs and standards and attitudes of mind would have to be discovered.

Hence the revolt against all customary ways. Hence the growing suspicion that a wealth of hidden power and untold experiences lie neglected within man himself. Hence, in order to forget outer sordidness and release inner possibilities, one drug after another has been resorted to. Finally, youth has fought its way to the discovery of the ancient Eastern knowledge of personal development. The age-old sciences of meditation and integration have been approached and tried out.

But with how much success? Up to the present it is not easy to find any adequate, responsible or correctly-adapted teaching on meditation and its relevant practices. For it is a subject which is at once subtle and simple, and simply subtle. Untold millions of words and hours of teaching have always been expended upon it in certain parts of the world—those parts, in fact, which have produced the most glorious cultures and lasting sciences. We all know of the inscription over the doors of the early Temples— 'MAN KNOW THYSELF'. This was indeed prophetic, for it is the last thing man can do, yet it is the first essential leading to any real achievement.

Standing *en masse* before this challenging inscription are the young people of today, demanding help, and representing for the first time the possibility of a regenerated world. For make no mistake! These are no ordinary youth, but a vast company of beings who have earned the right to build a new age, and have come to birth in order to do it. This right is being expressed by a refusal to be conditioned; by a determination to live their own way; by a searching appraisal of religion, education and working conditions.

Moreover this is the time when the world is moving into the Astrological Sign of Aquarius, giving us a set of stellar and cosmic conditions which release new influences and powers to flood us all. The response of each depends upon his state of development and awareness. But the power, the stimulation and the pressure is there. It draws forth a response from the very earth herself, who, like a giant atom, is reaching the stage of inner combustion when great changes will take place.

However, no matter what eventuates in the form of cataclysms, earthquakes, flying saucers, etc., the result will depend upon the response, understanding, efforts and ardency of individual men and women. Those who are able to seize the opportunity will begin to remake their world and model a new and utterly different civilisation.

One has only to look at these young people with clear eyes to see that they are, inherently, a new race of beings, having little in common with the crystallised, conditioned, apathetic and stupefied state of most of the older generation. Nevertheless, there do exist a certain number of the older generation who, ahead of time, have fitted themselves to understand and to live in the new-age ways; who are able to meet the new youth half-way, explain to them all that has been denied to them in their education, and link up with them to remodel world civilisation.

Which of the older ones are fortunate enough to belong in the new-age category? This is where we must search ourselves deeply, all of us of every age. For of course, physical age has nothing to do with it. It is a question of the age of the soul.

In this book we are going to outline this search for ourselves. We will prepare a thorough psychoanalysis, a 'do-it-yourself' which will enable the student to sort himself out at his own leisure, and clear his psychological decks for action and progress, and self-fulfilment.

Although our system may at first appear to be simple and primitive, it is *basic*. Rightly followed, it will lead up to an understanding of the most advanced of psychological teachings, such as Krishnamurti's, which leads us to the final breaking up and dissolving of the personality shell. This makes possible the phenomenon known as the 'second birth', which sets free the living individuality, the real man, undated, unconditioned, and ready for the new age.

Self-examination is a long and drastic process for those who have never attempted it and have had no practice.

For some it is far easier than for others. Yet 'slow and steady often wins the race'. And the goal ahead is release into freedom, that first freedom which itself provides a stepping-stone to the yet more intensive cleansing process practised by the Zen Buddhists. This latter certainly prepares students for the leap into a new civilisation, for it gives them the necessary mental nudity.

But there are many ways of examining the self! Either we can camouflage ourselves to ourselves, building up a false front and not facing ourselves frankly at all. Or else we can make every kind of excuse for anything too obviously wrong. Or else we can compare ourselves with other people who are 'so much worse than we' (although probably with far better excuse!) Or else we can dramatise ourselves with self-pity (a most destructive disease!) or else shelter under a convenient inferiority complex, which lets us out from using any initiative; a 'miserable sinner' rut which denies us the possibility of any achievement. Or else we can use the other side of the Inferiority coin, which is pride, and consider ourselves to be in the right, now and always! Even if we know better, we can do any of this so subtly that we can avoid recognising it.

However, none of it is going to get us anywhere at all—except backwards! There is only one key to the door of freedom and fulfilment, and that is honesty, integrity, the surrender to truth at all costs and the love of goodness for itself alone. It is this complete surrender, to God, to goodness, to change and growth, which is the door to achievement. When one loves God or good for its own sake, and intends to live for and within it; when one is ready to sacrifice one's career, security, comfort, connections and all else for it without a second thought! then, through that complete one-pointedness one will have conquered life, the world, and one's own destiny. Then miracles will begin to happen. Then one will learn to know what is worth while. Then one will attain that mysterious Power called Wisdom, and be enabled to wield it and live by it in the physical world.

Eventually one will move from darkness into light—and how can light be explained to those still in darkness, the darkness of an imprisoned mind? The 'second birth' into spiritual light is unexplainable. It is the transition into quite a different world, existing, nevertheless, in the same physical space! One has plugged oneself into light and power and knowledge, after having been as a little blind mole underground (even if outwardly a very successful business man!).

Is such an achievement worth while? If it is, then we must, with patience and determination, set forth on this initial voyage of discovery—the discovery of oneself.

WISDOM IN
PRACTICE

PART ONE

SELF-ANALYSIS

I

To Begin With, What Are We?

All around us the world of human affairs hums its busy complex life. The mixture of good and bad, beauty and sordidness, vitality and monotony, which offers itself for our judgement, is accepted by us according to our individual outlook. Perhaps we sometimes ask ourselves what the meaning is of this tantalising mixture, why it is as it is—maybe we criticise it all bitterly.

To what degree, though, do we connect it all with ourselves? Presumably, if we criticise, we do not hold ourselves in any way responsible. I would ask, then, whom or what do we consider responsible if we have to face the question?

Is it not true that the world of human affairs must mirror the sum total of the minds of humanity—that, in fact, it is even more than a reflection, for it is the actual creation built from men's motives in living?

A sum total is made up of units. Each unit is of such significance that the activity of even one of them may suffice to change the 'voting power', so to speak, of the whole. It follows, therefore, that we cannot claim that any one of us is without responsibility for the state of human affairs as we find it today. It follows, also, that any one of us might weigh down the balance which could either change or confirm that state. Moreover, it follows that by a careful analysis of a few *average* human beings we can discover what are the mental attitudes which have built and are building our world.

An analysis so searching can best be achieved by self-analysis, properly conducted. The two selves nearest to hand are those of the reader and the author. Therefore I suggest that we assume for the sake of our experiment that we are two *average* human beings (which we privately probably do *not* believe !). For the sake of putting a clear searchlight on to this vital subject of present world affairs I suggest that we make an unbiassed, honest and exhaustive study of ourselves, in so far as we are able. We can then try to determine if that which we find we *are* must and does result in the world being what it is today.

What will we have gained by this? Is it not of paramount importance to get clear the true causes of human failure, internationally, socially and economically? Instead of perhaps blaming God, the Devil, or other men, we might bring a full responsibility home to each one of us. This is indeed what I am hoping to prove with incontestible clarity—that you and I are responsible for the existence of that which such people as Hitler represented—and that, equally, we could be responsible for the creation of a new and lovely world.

If this fact could be brought home to us all, what dignity, what potentiality and what pride might be assumed by the least and most hopeless of us today ! It would be a challenge which would search out every one of us, for who can say which one will play the part of the final 'straw upon the hump of the camel' of 'Evil'?

If we can prove that the present world chaos and tragedy is the fault not of God, the Devil, capitalism or communism, but that it is *equally* shared, in various ways, by every living man, and exactly in what ways, we shall have a sound foundation on which to build. Having determined the causes, logic and common sense will indicate the cure.

Many people avoid the difficulty of thinking by turning away the subject with timeworn platitudes about religion. They say : 'People must learn to go back to God !' or : 'Men must learn to follow Christ !' or : 'They must become spiritual instead of materialistic !'

As to how all this is actually to be done they have usually nothing to add.

'Let God guide men' often means, 'Do not think for yourselves.'

The apparently deeply religious man has often been a cruel fanatic, a murderer and an oppressor. Or he has developed meanness, smugness and narrowness.

Evidently the fact of confessing ourselves religious, or even of being really in earnest, is not enough. We need something more. It is essential to know what that something is.

If we look, for instance, at the Christian religion we can select two suggestions. The first one is :

'Be ye wise as serpents and harmless as doves.'

It takes great wisdom to achieve harmlessness. The injunction seems to imply self-effort rather than the habit of allowing God to do the thinking for you, as so many would have it.

The second statement I would bring forward tells us that when we become as little children we shall know the Kingdom of Heaven. This certainly implies simplicity.

Wisdom and simplicity are therefore not in contradiction to each other, but must exist concurrently. Here, I think, is our first clue to failure, because modern life is anything but simple. Neither do we find simplicity within men's minds nor within our own. In fact our minds are so vaguely complex that many of the important things we have already mentioned may have no real meaning to us at all.

If things have gone all wrong with our lives someone will say : 'You should turn to God. . . .' Whether they know what they mean it would be difficult to find out. But their words may convey absolutely nothing to us. We may not believe in 'God'. Or, 'believing', we may achieve no definite impression within our minds at all.

If, on the other hand, it were suggested that we turn the clear light of analysis upon our lives, and through logical reasoning link up cause and effect, thus gaining simple proof of what is needed to put our lives to rights, I doubt if anyone would deny the possibility of help in this way.

Why, however, should not 'God' mean reasoning and logic? What ancestral inhibition prevents us from associating practical living with the Creator Who designed all? Why must we shut Him off into a separate sphere of nebulous 'power', 'love' and other vaguenesses? Surely a most practical and ingenious mind designed the Universe? There is nothing at all vague about That which keeps the fine balance of power and motion on which existence as we know it depends.

Therefore, if we in our small sphere are to make an essay in logic and reasoning and practical sense, do *not* let us assume that we are being 'unspiritual', whatever we mean by that. In relying on ourselves we are not leaving God out, since we are told that all is One, inseparable. The difference between spirituality and materialism must be defined. It is surely actually the difference between focusing one's interest on either the cause or the effect of all phenomena. Cause is powerful and lasting. Effect is evanescent and dependent. Cause is simple, its effects are multiple. Cause is 'God' in His eternal aspects. Effects are 'God' in His passing expressions. We have the choice either to associate ourselves with the eternal character and purpose of 'God' or with the effects of the changing phases incident to the development of this purpose. The first orientation we know as spirituality, the second as materialism. It is this occupation with incidentals which has divorced men from reality and therefore from practicality.

In this book we are out to find just how much each one of us is responsible for the state of human affairs today. If we can bring home the blame equally to all of us and ascertain our part in the creation of present world chaos, then by the same token we will have discovered the cure, and the means by which all of us without exception must build our new world. Human beings are living creatures with indefatigable urges towards self-preservation and propagation or family life. So also are plants, animals and insects. Yet there is a difference. It will be well to determine what human beings are as a species before we begin to analyse ourselves individually.

It is certain urges or motives which propel all life through the processes of evolution. So we must consider in what way the human life-motive differs from those of other living creatures. Speaking generally, we act because of what we believe. We sow seeds because we believe they will germinate; we have had proof of it. We study a profession because we believe that we will make our living by it; we have had proof of that also. We believe in other things, too, of which the tangible proof may be in question. We believe them because our parents or neighbours or ancestors believed them.

Every act and the energy of living itself must be backed by some more or less conscious belief which motivates our life-impulse. The life-impulse of a tiny seed is colossal in respect of its size. It sends forth a delicate plant tip which can pierce through earth hard enough to defy our spades. From where does that tremendous impulse come, that flow of force on tap from the universe through a tiny seed? How much greater is the life-urge tapped by you and me! It has ensured man's survival through any and every type of obstruction and destruction, even self-destruction.

Yes, the same life force is there in man, but whereas in the animal and plant it seems to be controlled by a serene and confident intelligence which ensures a steady and slow progress, in man the situation is different. We can see at once that man is very complex. He possesses in his primitive state the animal and plant nature which can imbue him with self-protective instincts. He also possesses that assumption of existing Divinity, that awareness of and interest in causes and powers behind form, which we call spirituality, and which for all we know may be shared by plant and animal as well. He possesses, also, the reasoning human brain, which we can assert is his alone, and is not used by any other form of life. We may even find arguments to show that superhuman beings, if they do exist, do not use, and have no need to use, a brain such as human beings have.

A human being is like a little walking nervous plexus, a little telephone exchange of many switchboards, a little wireless instrument receiving innumerable wave-lengths. So also are the animals and insects and plants, to an extent which we are only beginning to discover. But whereas the latter appear to be *unquestioningly* guided by these impressions, the human being subjects them to the reactions of his mentality, with a different result in each individual.

Under the scrutiny of the psychologist and the psychoanalyst our apparent complexity increases, the hundreds of influences to which we are subject, the inhibitions and habits to which we are slaves! The inference is that our lives are a series of rigid automatic reflexes. On the face of it, this can be proved to be the case. We are bound up in layers and layers of unthinking habit.

But what happens? A sudden emergency occurs, or an unusual stimulation, and we see this creature of automatic reflexes galvanised by *something* into an utterly different being, potent, independent, original, driven by some intelligent force within which is usually dormant.

How has this change come about? *Motive* has been aroused, either the motive to act according to the emergency, or according to the stimulation. Motive seems to act like light or heat; it produces change. It can change an inert, timid, habit-ridden nonentity into a powerful, violent, original, courageous, dynamic force, with tremendous influence. This has been done by some stimulation which has put in action a definite *motive* or ambition. People ascribe much to will-power, but that alone is obviously impotent and inoperative unless it is harnessed to a definite *motive*. Will-power cannot function without an ambition even if that ambition is to do nothing !

Plant and animal life are actuated by *instinctive* motives, those of growth, propagation and self-preservation. Man shares these in his natural state. But the complexities of his reasoning brain, and his *self-conscious* responses to unseen forces, furnish him with a variety of motives which have evolved civilisation as we know it today. It is not a man's knowledge which affects his actions and his life—it is the extent to which that knowledge has stimulated his motive-power. Let us get this quite clear. Whereas animals and plants express *collectively* the 'mind of nature', or the intelligence behind natural phenomena, man is the living expression of an individual ideal. It may be a very low ideal, but it is his own, and distinctly different from any other man's. This ideal is his life-motive, determining his whole development and career. This life-ideal may be so slight and unconscious as to be hardly perceptible. In fact there are some domesticated animals who have achieved more life-ideal than some men.

If you can sum up a person's innermost attitude to existence and thereby assess his motive in living, you will know the colour of his various ambitions and the length of time he will probably hold to them.

So far we have ascertained that the principal attribute of human beings, which can make everything or nothing of them, is this possession of an individual life-motive, and that everything turns individually and collectively upon the quality and force of that life-motive. Therefore the most important thing we can begin with in the analysis of ourselves is the study of our own life-motives.

Can you, for instance, say straight off what, in your inmost heart, you are living for? What you actually think of yourself and believe yourself capable of? If you wish to achieve this—and, if so, why? And, if not, why? Have you even considered what you actually are, and why you are in existence on this planet? Have you any belief about it, any conception that you have a part to play?

Will you try to clarify this question of your aim in life? Possibly it centres round home and family. You may love your family, and wish to protect, beautify and develop your home and give to its members the best chance in life. On the face of it, that seems to be a good and worthy life-motive. But frankly, it is one which we share with the animals, birds and insects, and in which we are, if anything, rather behind some of them as a whole. Nevertheless, we may declare that ambition in family life is sufficient for a life-motive. But is it? We may say that it is the 'backbone of a nation', forgetting that a backbone is not enough—an ape or a lunatic has a perfectly sound backbone. The Germans are very good at family life, but that did not prevent them from agreeing to take part in a very ugly page in their history.

No, let us get this clear. Family life is an animal instinct brought to greater perfection by some birds and insects than by man. We are casting no aspersion. Animals often show a love, a nobility of character, and a practicalness in family living that would render men godlike could they but emulate it. In speaking of animal instincts we refer to those qualities which were in being before men walked the earth, and which he himself contains plus his human qualities. To those human qualities, which are connected with the human brain, man has sacrificed many of his sound family instincts. We must consider what the exchange has brought him.

What does a human being bring to his family life to supplement the animal qualities of devotion, industry, instinct and courage? How closely, for instance, can you ascertain your own motives in regard to family life? Do you cherish your family because they are *yours*, your possession, something to feed your pride of ownership, or because they add to your comforts, provide you with a warm escape from the outer world, give you people with whom you can talk and be natural, or who look after your creature comforts? Do you cherish your children because they are going to be a credit to *you*, support you in your advancing years, because you can fulfil yourself in them and their achievements; or see them do the things you *might* or ought to have done yourself? Do you cherish your family because anything is better than loneliness, and because they give you a feeling of having a place in the world?

If these are your life-motives in regard to your family then, in your mind, they revolve around you—*you* are the centre of your stage, and you must confess yourself self-centred, with a horizon bounded by the walls of your home and the confines of your career. You may therefore belong in the first group, the animal-motived person, or in the second group, the self-centred person.

Perhaps, however, your ideals are more developed than this, and you hope to contribute to the welfare of mankind through the medium of your family. Possibly you are ambitious for them, wishing to produce famous children, not for wealth or reflected glory for yourself, but so that *you* will have created something socially helpful and valuable. If only you knew that your children will make good you would die happy.

But, please think, why should it matter more to you that *your* children do well than that anyone else's children do well?

Are you not still being self-centred, and seeking for self-justification and fulfilment?

'Oh, but that's ridiculous!' you say. 'Would you have me without pride or interest in my own children?'

I have known mothers with ten or twelve children who were able to love them each most passionately. If one of those mothers had had only one child and concentrated her heart upon it, although having the power to love so many, potential love would have been lost to ten other children while one received an excess of it. Whether you or I have children or not, we must assume that we are potentially able to love and care for many little ones. But if we do have one or two and concentrate all our parental love upon them, because *we* have brought them forth, we are limiting our own potentialities. We are cutting ourselves off from the wonder and interest of a whole world of children. We are trying, albeit unconsciously, to concentrate our child's interest upon ourselves alone, and limiting, through example, his own capacity for loving the rest of his generation.

'But,' you say, 'I cannot help especially loving my own child, because he resembles his mother—or his father, or our own parents—we have so much in common!'

This may be true in some cases, but actually not to the degree we think. Many children are astonishingly unlike their relatives;

or else the resemblance is mostly physical and superficial, or else
due to being cooped up with the family habits and ideas. Often
we could discover other people's children who would really bear
more resemblance in character to ourselves than do our own. An
enclosed family life certainly breeds sameness, and by the same
token dullness and monotony.

That tremendous injunction 'Love your neighbour as yourself'
must also surely mean 'Love your neighbour's children as your
own!' If everyone lived on this basis all children would get a
fairly equal share of love and care, even if their own parents
were not competent to give it. Instead of the few being pampered
into disease while the many were neglected into disease, the whole
standard of living would be evenly raised. The immediate effect
on your own child would be the advantage of healthier, happier
and more charming companions, and he would also be quick to
follow your lead.

We see at once, therefore, what a vital part possessiveness and
self-centredness in the home play in the whole structure of the
nation, purely from the individual standpoint and without the
interference of any outside authority at all.

Possessiveness and jealousy between parents, or from parent to
child, give the rising generation a wrong start in life from the
first. It is not really natural, which is proved by the fact that it
produces all sorts of inhibitions and unnatural results, such as
the mother-complex, the father-complex, the Oedipus complex,
and the inferiority complex.

A great many animals have a feeling of responsibility for all
baby creatures. Recently I saw a photograph of an enormous St.
Bernard dog who had brought home a minute baby rabbit to his
owners, which, being about the size of one of his toes, was seated
upon the dog's foot while he watched over it with great tender-
ness. Such responsibility is easily fostered in animals. They will
often mother those other than their own even if of quite a different species and their natural enemies—such as the cat discovered
the other day busily suckling some young rats!

It seems wise to realise that if our primary aim in life is centred
in our family, it will not necessarily be beneficial to them, to ourselves, or to the general community. It will depend on the extent
to which self-centredness colours this aim.

Let us suppose, however, that it is a career and not family

which fills the horizon of our ambitions. We want to make good. Why? In order to feed our family? to keep our parents? to be able to enjoy the good things of life? to justify ourselves? to become famous? to enforce our own positive idea or ideal? because we have been brought up to do so? to use up our insistent energy? to benefit humanity?

Our motives in building a career may range from the highest idealism, through the varied gamut of self-seeking, down to an unthinking automatic acceptance of the necessity for so doing. We may, in fact, discover that the whole range of these motives plays its part in our make-up. We may bring into our living a set of mixed motives for everything we do. This is indeed the case with many of us. Direct simplicity of motive is a rare phenomenon, and where it exists it will carry all before it.

It is not difficult to ascertain what our life-motive (or central underlying ideal) is if we consider our life and health as the index, because they are, of course, the exact reflection and creation of that motive. Mixed motives will produce a complex unharmonious existence, and a variety of discordances in the bodily health and functions. The strife within ourselves spreads outwards in ripples of influence and adds to all that makes for wars between the nations.

The world war had its beginning within us. It was originated by each one of us. We tried to fasten the blame on to the 'forces of evil', but their connection with ourselves was carefully ignored. In these pages we are going to face quite squarely just what those 'forces of evil' are, and where we all stand in relation to them.

We cry out against capitalism, against muddled authority, vested interests, an inefficient Church. We blame various things for our inadequate lives. But already this first chapter of frank reflection has shown us that we could be independent of much of all that if we started from the stronghold of our own homes to 'love our neighbour's children as our own', and founded our living upon a life-motive which worked for the good of the many instead of for the few or the one.

It is that same life-motive which rules the home which will guide the world. If it is self-centred it will create a world of separatism and conflict. If it is world-centred it will create a 'whole' world, unified and coherent.

Whence springs this so terribly important motive-power, in the last analysis?

It springs, surely, from the fount of our belief—from that which we actually accept, believe and understand about the purpose and meaning of all life, and which gives us our motive in living. Your faith and mine are helping to run the world at this time.

How much do we know, then, about that all-important faith? In what do we believe?

Presumably we belong to one or the other of the orthodox religions. It is usually arranged for us that we belong to some faith. We must admit that these religions, faulty though we may find them in some ways, have been built up for us with endless patience, self-sacrifice and devotion throughout many generations. If people find them crystallised or lifeless at this time, they are quick to blame orthodoxy for their own lack of faith and interest. They forget that the shortcomings of the Church are the shortcomings of men, and of men drawn from their own ranks. They forget that the energy and life-blood of the Church must be supplied by themselves. If they do not do their share of thinking and play their own part, their Church will be drained of life. If they prefer to be impressed by pomp and circumstance, then pomp and circumstance is all they will get.

Where do you and I stand in this vital matter of belief—this springboard of all our actions? Are we convinced that there is a purpose and a goal behind the existence of these teeming millions of little human beings? Do we believe in a Great Intelligence directing and designing the life around us to fit some grand scheme? Do we accept the 'God' of our parents automatically and unthinkingly as Someone conveniently there, to be appealed to for help in moments of blind difficulty? To many the Creator is a vague great personality, human in type, perpetually to be asked for help in their minute personal spheres, and occasionally to be thanked for favours and protection. Such people seem content eternally to remain in the position of serfs or children *vis-à-vis* their Creator, and never to attain adulthood and an attitude of responsibility and co-operation at all. When their own children treat them in exactly the same way they miss the inference of imitation, and feel aggrieved.

Perhaps, however, you and I belong among those who have

passed from 'orthodoxy' in religion to those conditions of personal application to truth which go under the names of occultism, mysticism, theosophy, spiritualism and so on. We may thus
have made an individual effort to discover more, to believe more.
We may have perhaps absorbed a tremendous amount of
theoretical teaching, acquainted ourselves with a variety of
phenomena, developed new capacities on our own account. We
may have passed from the ranks of the taught into those of the
seeker. We may feel superior—or more fortunate, as the case may
be. We may have embraced the vision of the Deity of Deities, of
the great Plan for the Universe, of the mighty wheel of evolution
whereon we swing and have our decisive part to play. We may
have heard of all this and accepted these things in our minds.

But still—what do we *believe*?

We can only ascertain what we believe by the results, in our
lives and in our health, and not by the lip-service we do to a set
of conceptions, theories or teachings.

If we really believe in a God of love and justice and a brotherhood of men, in the individual working out of our own salvation,
in the evolution towards perfection of all life—if we really believe
even a little in these things then we shall find ourselves beginning
to lose hate, worry, envy, greed, possessiveness, lethargy, complexity, and the diseases brought about by all of these states.

If we take any interest in the wonderful work, the mysterious
purpose and the marvellous intelligence in activity all around us,
our extreme attention will be shifted from little personal and
physical concerns. Death and suffering will have a quite different
meaning for us. Our life-motive will have changed out of all
recognition. Our minds will have escaped from the cramped
prison of a one-celled existence into the free vault of heaven and
the universal Intelligence. Because we have learnt to believe in
the Whole, we can think and act for the whole instead of for
the micro-cell (ourselves). Our life-motive will be to live for the
many in accordance with the Plan, and any lesser ambition will
be submerged within it.

This is not to say that we cannot be faithful workers for our
home, our country, and our church. On the contrary, as we bring
to each detail of our work our vision of the Whole, we can invest
each small activity with an intenser interest and purpose. If it is
to the Divine Interest that every fly and microbe goes through

left their rulership to a few individuals. Decadence sets in when, the initial stimulation of empire-building once over, the life-motive of the nation weakens, and she sinks back to feed upon her colonies and go soft at the core.

This deterioration is due to the collective deterioration of her natives, one and all. It is a failure which we must bring home to ourselves. If the British Empire is not to go the way of so many others we must bring in a new element in history, otherwise history will repeat itself. This new element could develop from the British Commonwealth of Nations.

Are we content to believe all that our politically-inspired history books tell us, and ignore all that they leave out? Do we submit to having our minds poured into a mould designed to produce obedient, patriotic unquestioning servants of the state?

It is splendid to give love and loyalty to one's country. This does not, however, constitute a blind obstinate insistence that one's country cannot do and has never done anything wrong or mistaken. Love in its essence is *understanding,* and that involves clear, unbiased seeking. Loyalty in its essence is *helping,* actively and with all the intelligence at one's command. It includes standing out firmly against any national activity which is unworthy. True patriotism is responsibility, and consists in seeking not that one's country shall gain the best, but that it shall give the best to the rest of the world.

Let us see how our own patriotism measures up to this standard. If it is agreed that patriotism is necessary to ensure the very life-blood and existence of our nation, it follows that while half of our love and energies might reasonably go into the building up of our homes and family life, the remaining half should be the least we must give to the support of our nation.

Do we give this?

How much of our strength, our devotion and our wits do we actually and deliberately devote to the studying and helping of our life as a nation?

'Oh, well,' you say, 'that's a tiresome question! I am a civil servant—or a farmer—or a barrister—or an M.P.—naturally all my work *does* help the nation!'

The motive which fires your work will make of it an asset or a liability to your country, and not the ostensible purpose of it. Your work may be of national importance—yet to you it may not have that significance at all, but be merely a means to an end, and that end financial security. War is a criminal catastrophe (in actuality), yet there are those who hope that it will continue because it provides them with a good job. This is purely callous opportunism, yet those very people can deceive themselves by calling it patriotism. Here is a dangerous example of mixed motives.

If human beings compromise through mixed motives their collective attitude as a nation will be the same. Hitler was enough of a psychologist to know this. He thus counted on an indefinite attitude towards right and wrong, a tortuous indecision due to self-interest, a lack of concerted harmonious action between nations who were unharmonious and unconcerted within themselves and their individual nationals. He worked to stimulate every German with the exact type of patriotism which suited his plans, and welded them into a concerted whole and proved what colossal strength such unified opinion and purpose can give. That this purpose was that of national self-interest and greed, was a great misfortune and waste of opportunity.

Possibly if the Germans had done more individual thinking and developed the responsibilities of true patriotism of which we have been speaking, they would not have been such easy prey for mass hypnotism, and could not have been imbued with the blind crude fanaticism which sometimes masquerades under the title of patriotism. They might have encouraged Hitler to nobler efforts, of which he had shown himself capable.

However, we must remember that we are still at the first stage of our exploration, which is that of self-analysis. Touching upon national history has brought us within range of the subject of education, so we can next discover where we stand in this all-important sphere. What is our attitude towards education? Do we regard it with distaste, as a tiresome obligation, a dull necessity, belonging to a short period in our youth, to be got through somehow, and put behind us with relief? Do we regard it through the spectacles of an inferiority complex, doubting our own abilities, fearing the effort we may have to expend, and resenting the hours of sunlight spent cramped at a desk? Perhaps, nevertheless, we are ready to put up with all this for the sake of getting on in the world, or to please our parents and become a 'credit' to them. We may even find our studies interesting in themselves, and we may crave the sense of power and superiority which learning brings. Or we may have an innate love of knowledge for its own sake, and an absorbing interest in certain—or various— aspects of life.

We may study under coercion of some kind—or because we like it—or to fulfil a personal ambition—or for all three reasons. Finally, we may be filled with a longing to serve our fellow-men, and seek knowledge as a means of so doing.

Whatever may be our individual attitude towards education it must go towards the production of future teachers, their systems and their pupils. If the tremendous importance of the teacher's work is not appreciated, apathy will be brought to bear on it from all sides—from pupil, parents, educational authorities, government, and the teachers themselves. It may be that your lethargy and mine towards this subject spreads its influence and may infect not only the pupils of the next generation, but people who will have tremendous influence on the whole trend of educa- tion. Remember, it is the weight of a hair that finally turns the scales.

Supposing that we regard education as a system of filling the brain with facts, and consider that our only active part in our own education is to memorise these facts and be able to produce them like a rabbit out of a hat if ever they are required! Sup- posing that in our schools we shirked our work, leaving it as late as possible to cram facts into our brains just before an examina- tion. Has not education thus been used for making of us a kind of card index rather than developing in us the power to think, to reason, and to create original ideas? And have we not been con- tent to allow this to be so for the very reason that we did not have to make the effort of creative thinking, but merely learnt up our collection of facts, in order to depend upon them like a row of crutches, from which we dare not move lest we fall down?

Practically the only thing that our education demanded of us was memory. If we shirked even a little, our memory became bad, but if we were keen students, to that degree we developed excel- lent memories. We relied upon them for use, profit and entertain- ment. This gave us a tendency to dwell in the past, our memories became precious to us, and to some of us they constitute the whole richness of our lives. We expend a vast amount of brain energy in constantly remembering and remembering, both things important and details of no importance at all. We are the slaves of memory to the extent that many of us actually believe that to remember is to think.

Thus to many of us the actuality and process of thinking has no meaning. We are ignorant of its quality, as a blind man is ignorant of colour. The fact that the future is as important, or more so, than the past, and deserves equal expenditure of brain energy, is a point that we may shirk, because to consider the future needs more than memory. Here memory is no longer a useful crutch—we have to stand alone and we have to think. Even to consider the future purely for amusement we have to deduce, imagine, create. As for considering the future from a constructive point of view, with the normal wish (which should surely be everyone's) to offer some idea, plan, improvement or other contribution to it—this takes real thought, and makes of each one of us a potential pioneer and a human factor worthy to be taken into account.

There may be said to be two ranks of human beings—those who think and those who do not think. It is not easy to determine this division until we are sure that we ourselves know what thinking is!

'But, good gracious!' you exclaim, 'I'm forever thinking—I think all day long—I can't help it, I've so much to worry about!'

Quite so, but is that exactly thinking? If we are worrying about ways and means, of how to manage our time or our money or reach our objective, we are reasoning along much the same lines as the ape when he puts one box upon another in order to reach a banana. There are those who argue that animals think, and there are those who hold that all their actions are done 'by instinct', whatever that means. If that is so, the latter might just as well say that all our efforts to manage our domestic lives, to obtain food and covering, or the means to buy them, are made 'by instinct' also.

Perhaps they are! It would suit my argument, anyway, which is that the divine power of creative thought which is available to man alone, is hardly brought into use in the average life of today. Part of his actions and thought processes are due to 'instinct'; part are due to habits taught to him in his youth, and the rest are a kind of imitation or reflection of all that goes on around him.

Let us search our own minds for a really original thought, plan or conception. If we are asked our opinion about a certain subject, we will either discover that we do not have one, or we will trot out from memory the views expressed by some person or publication with which we find ourselves congenial. An opinion in most cases consists in finding someone else's opinion with which we can agree. We shamelessly adopt it as our own, and it seems quite natural to us to give it as our own personal conclusion the next time we are consulted on that subject.

Now, this is not thinking, is it? It is not really very much more than a parrot does. There are many who declare that a parrot knows what he is saying. On the other hand, I have heard human beings express very vigorously a second-hand opinion, and when it came to the point they did not understand what they were talking about at all, having never given their minds to the subject.

Such folk would be 'dead against communism' or 'all for democracy', yet if you asked them clearly to define these words, they would be thoroughly annoyed, and largely incompetent to do so.

The moment any one of any type begins really to think for himself he becomes original, he becomes like a little power station, and things begin to happen and come to life in his vicinity. Perhaps people follow his lead, or perhaps he inspires others to do things. Maybe he will utter just one sentence, which is repeated, and finally finds its way into the mind of a man capable of altering the course of history, and inspires him to do so. This is something, you will agree, which can never be done by an animal, and a person who never does it never really rises above the animal state.

Where do you and I stand, most of us, in respect of our divine prerogative of dynamic creative thought? How many thoughts have we which have contributed something essential to human progress? If we are good Christians, how many words and actions (concrete thoughts) of ours have helped to further the Christian ideal? If we are good patriots then how much original thinking have we contributed towards the development of our national character, example and achievement? If we cannot bring home to ourselves any definite contribution in these respects, then we *are* neither patriots nor Christians; we are merely imitative reflections of environing influences.

If you were to search yourself clearly and mercilessly would you discover that you are only an imitative reflection? That is the crucial question. It is a most uncomfortable thought, but it is something we have to face if we are to achieve the goal aimed at in this book. For if we are but imitative reflections instead of actively thinking men and women, and if we leave the running of this world to other imitative reflections, hoping that there may be someone amongst them with enough 'go' to get something done—then it is a wonder that the world is not in a worse muddle than it is.

Looked at in this light we can see at once that the world at present is in fact obviously built on a number of unconnected imitative reflections, mostly of things long outlived, and all trying vainly to compromise between each other. Our world is us, is as we make it—every one of us. Until we each take up our full individual responsibility we shall continue making fools of ourselves, and ignoring the most wonderful potentialities of our existence.

3

Our Morality

We have briefly considered our attitude towards home, career, religion, country and education. Probably the thing next in importance to analyse will be our morality. Firstly, whether we have any definite moral standards; secondly, whether we keep to them. There has, as we all know, been rather a revulsion towards standards of morality during the last score of years or so, and by morality we mean those standards of behaviour which we set up or which are set up for us in respect of all our actions.

In a cruder, earlier civilisation standards were rigid and punishment was harsh. You could be hung for stealing a sheep, and if you were interested in anything new or unusual, such as witchcraft, astronomy, science or medicine, you were liable to be burnt at the stake. During this period sex morality harboured a mass of contradictions. While it was rigid in some aspects, in others it was most lax. For instance, it is said that for some generations much of the Italian aristocracy were built up from illegitimate children of the popes. The *droit du seigneur*—or the right of the squire of the village to possess the village maidens before their marriage—would be a case for the law today.

Standards governing sex behaviour have varied enormously according to period and climate. Standards governing other behaviour have varied much less all over the world, but have been ignored or circumvented to an amazing degree. The subject of morality is a widely spreading one, with many side issues. To find our way in its labyrinths we must first define a few fundamentals to which to cling. By fundamentals I mean those few rock-bottom moral standards which are essentially the same all over the world wherever an advanced state of development exists.

If we begin with the Christian faith, we can take only two; for instance : 'Do unto others as you would that they should do unto you', and 'Thou shall love thy God (or good) with all thy heart, and with all thy mind, and with all thy soul' (no mixed motives!). It is not difficult to see at once that if only these two commands were obeyed ideal human living would be assured. We can agree, also, without much difficulty, that these two commands exist in their essence in all other great religious faiths.

Directly we consider the variations in human faiths, we find that they are man-made. The more variations there are the more man has tampered with the purity of the original.

As an example let us consider our marriage laws. Christ said 'Whom God has joined together let no man put asunder.' 'God' was synonymous with 'love', and it is true that so long as two people really love they will not seek divorce, they will not be fundamentally unfaithful, and they will resist separation. Man, however, substituted the priesthood for God or love, and proceeded to declare that a priest-made marriage must be adhered to no matter how immoral or degrading it turned out in actuality to be. When divorce laws were instituted they were often so designed that they brought even greater degradation and unpleasantness into the relationships of sex.

Latterly, as the human spirit expanded and became more independent, the ideal of 'free love' appeared. From rigidity and imprisonment within sex restrictions people went to the extreme of promiscuity and flippancy, especially in the newer countries.

All these complications come, of course, from the mixed motives of those who made the laws and those who broke them. The issues are really simple if we can keep to fundamentals. If we were always to consider the feelings and well-being, both at the time and for the future, of any potential partner-in-love with the same earnestness and conscientiousness that we should apply to ourselves, we should be shown the ideal way in any circumstances. Since, however, some of us do not spend any real consideration on our own health and happiness and future, but just grab whatever we can get or fancy at the time, and refuse to bring a vision of the whole issue to the situation at all, we make a bad start. If we have so little regard or intelligence to apply to ourselves, it is not surprising that we have not much to put at the service of others.

We must obviously begin with ourselves, hence the oldest commandment of all : 'Man, know thyself !' Yet many people have been so extraordinarily half-witted that if they do wish to reform themselves and live according to spiritual laws, they usually develop a gigantic sin-complex. They deny and frustrate and thwart many of their natural instincts without the slightest attempt to understand them. Thereby they saddle themselves with a load of inhibitions which have the opposite effect on their character to the one they are seeking.

To a number of people morality consists in not being found out. They endeavour to conceal much of what they actually think and do, not only from others but from themselves. If they thus refuse squarely to face themselves they deny to themselves the opportunity of gaining a first-hand knowledge of a human being, and are therefore ill-equipped to understand and help those most near to them—husband, child or friend.

In thinking of morality we should remember that it is really only one single quality, although it bears different aspects in regard to varied subjects such as education, politics, sex and business. In its fundamental essence, however, morality really means having an active responsibility towards one's fellow men, and treating them in all ways as one would wish oneself to be treated, as well as all the other kingdoms in Nature.

This would entail a care to give full value for everything we get, and to take nothing which would deprive or handicap another, nor which is more than our proportionately fair share. This maxim could be applied, as you can easily see, to every activity of life. It would eliminate theft, usury, physical violence of all kinds, capitalistic tyranny, national tyranny, snobbishness, clannishness, and a thousand other kinds of selfishness and self-centredness, and exploitation in any sphere.

If we carefully apply this one standard to all our own moral reactions we shall maybe get some surprises about ourselves. For instance, whereas we might shrink in horror at the idea of stealing the smallest trinket from one of our friends, we may consider it perfectly legitimate to waste or steal his time, discouraging him from his studies for the sake of his company; or to steal his virtue or his honour, either by our own example or actions or by amusing ourselves by introducing him to bad companions; or to steal his chances in life through subjecting him to a harsh business deal; or to push him into the background so that our own social light shines unrivalled; or to deprive him of his right to needed human sympathy through our personal dislike, prejudice or intolerance.

There are so many different ways of stealing that go unreproved. All these different ways, multiplied by our neighbours, produce, of course, a collective dishonesty which may make of us a predatory or a robber nation. Where the self is the *only* consideration the vilest crimes can result. Where the self is the first consideration a predatory condition of selfishness is set up which results in slums, poverty, worry, fear, drudgery, ignorance and under-development, and poisoning of air, soil and water.

Obviously the first of these cases can apply to any aggressor state, while the second can apply to the more peaceable countries who still possess poverty and slums, soil erosion, etc.

It is time now clearly to analyse our own position in regard to this question of morality. We must determine whether we throw our weight among the getters or the givers; whether our chief and *first* concern is to obtain all the things which we consider necessary to our own comfort; whether we enjoy dispensing generosity *after* we have supplied ourselves or before. Do we ever go without so that a neighbour may have a share? Do we help to get someone else's work appreciated before we push forward our own? Do we encourage another's conversation and 'bring him out', subduing our own egotistical wish for self expression?

Unless we can measure up to these requirements we shall definitely be guilty of theft and oppression in subtle form sooner or later.

Surely what we have said here bears rather a terrible implication. We, who live respectable family lives, who hold solid positions in our community, who give regularly to church and flag day—*we* guilty of theft and oppression?

'Oh, I don't think I like this book! Fancy being called a thief! A perfectly horrible idea—and no one else would dream of thinking it about me!'

It does not signify in the least what other people think about us—or believe they think. In their innermost intuitions they will know the truth, and one day disappoint us terribly by their treatment of us. What matters is the truth, that truth which will bring to our thoughts and actions the inevitable results according to irrevocable natural and spiritual laws. What matters is that even our most private thoughts and actions, performed in the hidden corners of our private houses, go swinging instantly right round the world on the ethers, affecting all life as they go to an extent we cannot gauge.

Once we have sent them forth we cannot call them back and we stand convicted and responsible. A thought of hate may race away to swell a despot's power. A thought of impurity may help to urge the keeper of a brothel in his callous work. A thought of unkind criticism may determine a stranger's suicide.

With customary hypocrisy, materialism and ignorance, some people do not accept, do not wish to acknowledge these responsibilities, although science does more every day to prove to us that they are true. Electrical and radiatory sciences have shown us beyond question the speed and distance which sound and pictorial impressions can travel. From earliest history we have known that men's thoughts and appearances can be projected equal distances and speeds without instruments other than the human mind. We know also that a thought applied deliberately by the will can have powerful effects.

Yet we are as a rule too apathetic even to grasp these proved realities. We continue to sow the ethers with thoughts of envy, fear, resentment, loneliness, criticism and dislike, in blank defiance of the fact that they are not and cannot be our private thoughts. Not only do they affect our neighbours in a detrimental manner, but they are wide to the gaze of whatever discarnate Being or Beings we believe in—or Who exist whether we believe in Them or not.

If once we realise that our imagined privacy of thought has no existence, and that we are held as responsible for our thoughts as for our actions, it should help us very largely to eliminate our mixed motives. The only person they deceive is oneself—and then only one's outer physical self, the inner self being merely made unhappy.

This fact of the non-privacy of thought was clearly pointed out by Christ in His dissertation on the Ten Commandments. He explained that the crime of murder included also the mere hating of a man, or the calling of him 'thou fool!' and that those who 'slept with a woman in their minds' had as much as committed adultery. He could not have declared this great truth more plainly.

Do not, however, let us be depressed by these implications. Inasmuch as good is held to be in the long run more powerful than evil, we are free to do inexhaustible and wonderful good by thinking kind, understanding and encouraging thoughts, by thinking about others, in fact, as we would have them think about us.

So once more our argument comes home again to this one golden rule. We can apply it to our self-analysis.

How much good is done by the thoughts we give to those we know or know about? Will these thoughts bring out the best in them, encourage them so to act that this world will be a better place? Can we think about those who do not belong to us and who do not minister to our interests, and with whom we have 'nothing in common', with as much love and hope and understanding, as we have for our own dear ones?

Can we? *Can* we?

'If ye love them that love ye what merit have ye? Even the Pharisees do so!' Christ was tolerant about all sorts of sins, but not about mixed motives, which found their full expression in the hypocrisy of the Scribes and Pharisees. He poured His scorn upon them because they neither were honest in goodness nor wickedness, but tried to curry favour in both Heaven and Hell at the same time, thereby creating confusion. He was most lenient and forgiving of the more straightforward sins, which are often the result of a generous nature. We cannot imagine Him condemning, as we do, a poor man to six months' hard labour for stealing a loaf for his starving family. We can, however, picture Him being revolted by a blackmailer or slanderer.

Christ was far more tolerant of physical weakness than of evil and unkind thinking. Yet Christianity, because of people's preoccupation with the senses, has over-stressed the sin-sense in sex matters, to the detriment of the sin-sense about thought and speech, which is not nearly sufficiently developed. In other words, if we brought more care and understanding to our way of thinking the rest would look after itself.

'As a man thinketh in his heart so is he.'

These jewels of speech are talismans to happiness could we but give them the study they merit. Their simplicity deceives the muddled thinking due to our mixed motives.

If only we could make a quite new start with our conceptions of morality, make a clean sweep of all our old ideas, and set our minds free so that they can move forward into the new ways of thought which the processes of human evolution are to bring to us!

The great secret of originality, of freedom, of creativity, of progress and of success is to be able to empty the mind of the vast accumulation of ready-made or crystallised thoughts and conceptions with which it has been steadily filled during our lives.

To empty the mind! The Zen Buddhists train their pupils to cast out all thoughts, even the most brilliant and noble ones. The various systems of Meditation are planned to the same end. Psychoanalysis at its best frees the mind from a load of hoarded impressions and rigid thought-forms which completely impede the mind.

We have been told that in the service of Christ is perfect freedom, and that His yoke is light to bear. He explained to us that in singleness of motive, of vision and of ideal comes enlightenment. 'If thine eye be single thine whole body shall be full of light.'

If we could make a clearance of all our old ideas of morality and concentrate on the one fundamental principle—'love thy neighbour as thyself', and do that as our way of thanks to the Creator of all beauty and all possibilities—then should we indeed become powerful units in the building of a new and lovely world of men.

If we could each of us make a decision to begin with ourselves and learn to rule our own minds, and completely to bridle them, placing the reins under the control of the great Christian standard of love, all our present problems would melt away before us.

This sounds very simple, almost trite. But have we really thought about it? Does it in its beautiful simpleness elude our understanding?—or do we not *want* to understand it?

The establishment of such an inclusive love of all God's created world would mean that all its riches, pleasures and opportunities *would* be equally shared by all; that poverty, oppression, misery, disease, ignorance and slaughter *could* disappear in large measure from our midst, and that life would be so changed as to be hardly recognisable.

Do not let us promptly label this ideal of things being equally shared by all as 'socialism' or 'communism'! It need bear no labels except those of common sense, expediency and justice.

Do not let us say: 'Human nature will never change', or 'If you shared everything out equally, within a week someone would be top dog and profiteering would begin!' We might be accused of wishful thinking, or not *wanting* things to change because it would entail our having to change too.

There is already so much goodness, so much readiness for progress, so much patience and sacrifice and energy (wasted at present most needlessly) in the world that a little less apathy and a little more dedication and effort from a few of us might be enough to set in motion a tremendous reaction against the old selfish ways and uncover the wonderful potentialities lying just beneath their surface.

4

Our Inhibitions

If, as we have declared, there are such splendid potentialities within us, what is holding us back? Why cannot we be as we would like to be, as we really know that we ought to be?

It seems that we are held back by a collection of feelings and thought-habits which have been named 'inhibitions'. To inhibit is to forbid or prevent. Inhibitions, therefore, are things which restrain us from natural expression. Let us try to form a clear idea about them.

Supposing you suffer a temporary injury to your foot, which makes you limp at the time. You may carelessly continue this habit of limping after the injury is cured. You may thus give yourself a permanent limp. This may lead to adhesions in your muscular tissue, which will eventually bring on neuritis, or some form of 'rheumatism', and will later affect the spine, causing perhaps curvature and finally tuberculosis! For, once the natural harmony and rhythm of the human frame is upset, the repercussions will be far-reaching. In some people a fault in the feet will lead to defects in the eyesight or hearing. The symptoms may vary but the disharmony will affect the whole person.

The same law applies to the mind. A mental shock or injury may be received, and it will cause for a time a mental 'limp' such as a fear or prejudice. If we are careless this mental limp will be established as a permanent one and may throw the whole framework of our minds out of gear.

Besides this, mental and bodily symptoms are interchangeable. A mental limp may create a bodily one, and vice versa.

We will probably take it for granted that we have none of these mental limps, and that our minds are both normal and full of common sense.

But let us see.

Are we opinionated? Have we prejudices—for or against nations, communities, families, individuals, religions, politicians? What is a prejudice? It is a fixed thought which we do not wish to change, which we even choose to believe we *cannot* change. A prejudice is something which limits our thoughts. Selfless love of anything is not a prejudice because it seeks always to understand, and therefore is bound to enlarge the vision indefinitely. Possessive love *is* a prejudice because it seeks to limit its object within a narrow personal circumference and is therefore jealous and afraid of any enlargement of vision.

Patriotism can be a prejudice if it is possessive patriotism which would belittle the rights and qualities of countries other than its own. Religion can be a prejudice if it is a possessive religion, and this actual prejudice in religion has led to more cruelty and bloodshed than almost anything else in history.

So we see that the greatest things in life, if prejudice is applied to them, become utterly defiled.

Prejudice is another word for conscious inhibition.

We have been told quite a lot about the unconscious inhibitions. We know that they are fixed impressions or thought-habits so ancient and deep-seated that they have sunk below the threshold of memory and awareness. The psychoanalysts have explained to us that many of these thought-habits have been fixed into the depths of our characters by something that occurred in earliest childhood. Such deep mental shocks or wounds leave mental adhesions or warpings in the recesses of the mind, which in later youth may produce their results in the form of physical symptoms such as hysteria, fits, convulsions, obsessions and anaemia.

A clever psychoanalyst can completely eradicate these symptoms if he can bring to light the long-forgotten cause. If no psychoanalyst or other physician is called in, and no cure is attempted, a warped and distressing life may be the alternative. Even the psychoanalyst may not be very successful, because his treatments have sometimes been so extremely painful and agonising, in a mental sense, to the patient, that he has left fresh mental wounds in the place of those he has cured.

It may seem at first thought most unfair that some incident in childhood outside our own volition may thus deeply affect the course of our life and careers. It would appear to be a bad handicap to human progress. Yet, actually, these things need not take place at all. They are only further striking examples of the widespread results of our wrong methods of thinking and of upbringing.

From his earliest years the child is taught to obey, to store and hoard impressions, to memorise, but *not* to express his opinions, deductions or the impressions which he receives. The child questions the adult (being answered only according to the latter's mood and patience) but rarely does the adult question the child, and almost never with the idea of learning something from him. The child is thus usually thrown back within himself. He knows that he must 'keep quiet', and that adults will accept his confidences with amusement or in an admonitory attitude. The child's whole introduction to life is shadowed by the word 'don't!' The first formations within his character are repressions of various sorts.

Therefore when a small child receives some great shock or fright or dramatic experience, this repressive training and the already over-developed feeling of guilt cause him to drive down these powerful impressions deeply within himself. Thus this event in the baby's life, instead of undergoing natural examination and 'digestion', and adding richly to his conscious experience, in the give and take of outward expression to others, goes underground. There, as an explosive, thwarted quantity, it ferments, and as all fermenting things do, it undergoes complete changes in character, and appears upon the surface years afterwards as an unrecognisable symptom of some obscure disharmony.

For instance a child may be rescued from a burning house, and in the height of her terror may have involuntarily noticed a white shoe fallen upon the dark floor. Afterwards she asks many questions but the 'grown-ups' snub her—they want her to forget the experience, or to forget it themselves. Her terror and her questions sink back unsatisfied, and no one knows of her secret sufferings, which she finally forgets herself.

Years afterwards she is subject to unaccountable fits at long intervals. All fail to notice that the sight of a white shoe lying separately upon the floor will bring these fits on. The young girl is faced with a badly handicapped life.

If the simple law of love—'Do unto others as you would wish them to do unto you'—had been followed, the little child's questions would have been scrupulously answered and her own impressions drawn out. An amount of suffering, expense and difficulty would thus easily have been averted.

The psychoanalysts have uncovered for us a world of mystery, a realm of the deepest seeming complexities, in which our inner-most beings are apparently rooted and enmeshed, and before which we all stand nonplussed. Yet the simple law of love has an answer for all this. The word 'love' has, however, like many words, been so misused that to most of us it means no more than possessive attraction or affection. To others it means emotional sentimentalism. Yet the real original meaning of love is *wisdom*, because unselfish love (which is really the only love there is) brings a truer understanding and enlightenment than anything else.

So when we entitled this book *Wisdom In Practice* we really meant *The Practice of Love*. But thought-habits have invested the word with such inferior meanings that we could not use it without explanation. Therefore, when we speak of love in this book we refer to the real thing only, that deep unselfish outgoing radiance that seeks light and gives light to all around. This is the selfless impersonal love, as compared with the cheaper personal possessive love which is but an inferior imitation.

Thus a love which offers to little children full understanding and expression would suffice to do away with a large measure of physical and mental imperfection, and would therefore tremendously raise the health standard of the race.

It is as simple as that.

Apart from the many unconscious inhibitions, there are, of course, the conscious ones. In these cases, circumstances have driven a set thought or conception into the head like the hammer drives the nail. Parents often hammer nails thus into the heads of their children, purely to suit their own interests, which are, so it seems to them, that their children should be an echo of them-selves.

'The Jews are bad people.'

'Why, Daddy?'

'Oh, everyone *knows* they are !'

'But *why*, Daddy?'

'Because *I* say so! I know better than you and you should take Daddy's word for it.'

Or :

'Vested interests are the ruin of us all!'

'Why, Mummy, what are they?'

'Oh—er—you'll know when you're older! But remember: always hate the capitalist—he wants to suck your blood!'

'What is a capitalist?'

'Oh, a man with lots of money—don't ask any more questions!'

'But, *please* Mummy—Daddy says *I'm* to make lots of money when I grow up. . . . ?????'

'I'm sure I hope you will—now go away and play at once!'

Do we realise the foundations for thought which this kind of talk lays in embryonic minds, in their thousands and tens of thousands? It produces a set of people growing up who have been trained to think of a subject in terms of one hackneyed sentence, to limit and imprison it within that sentence, and to be content so to do. Life therefore becomes reduced to a set of phrases. Every subject is represented by one or two sentences which are clung to with the assumption that to seek for further meaning is awkward, unnecessary, dangerous, unseemly and strange.

We can all of us recognise some of the more obvious of these phrases for what they are, and we call them clichés or platitudes. It is a pity that we cannot also recognise that we have been inclined to treat all the wonders of life in that way, and to make of living one long never-ending platitude, so that we might just as well be marionettes for most of our day.

'Good morning! . . . How did you sleep? . . . It's colder today. . . . Quite a decent day, though. . . . Cheerio! . . . See you later!'

Laconic. Habitual. Half-conscious.

And this in the midst of a world of palpitating wonder, of ceaseless miracle! Every plant, insect, microbe—the changes of climate and atmosphere, every new endeavour of man, all his ancient achievements, the mystery of the far-flung universe, the fascination of all the vast mechanisms which supply us with what are supposed to be our essential needs—all this is full of ever-changing drama, of an amazing wealth of impressions for all our senses.

What does it all mean to us? Many of us are so completely *inhibited* that we are hardly alive. Everything in us has been successfully repressed, tied up, battened down. Our marvellous senses have become crude and half-functioning. We are imprisoned in a hard shell of habit and repression to such an extent that we are cut off from most of the beneficent radiations which flow to us from all life around.

Our 'receivers' are blunted, choked, non-functioning. We are starved, famished, and we become the prey to blind craving, which we attempt to satisfy in crude ways, by taking 'stimulants' or narcotics in their various forms. We know so well what these are—drink, meat, tobacco, drugs, sex, cheap fiction or drama, or some form of 'politics' or belief which stimulates us to antagonisms or fanaticisms. When once we are inhibited from the subtle pleasures which are our birthright, we get caught in a vicious circle indeed, and disharmony reigns within our minds and bodies.

What is this birthright of ours whose loss is such a disaster? It is just one thing—love, impersonal love, that force which gives us the desire to *understand*, which at once opens the mind. It is the wish to give, and repression melts before it.

As we are seeking for a quite fresh comprehension of life, we should begin with this word 'love', because its existence and its understanding determine the whole tenor of our lives and our contribution to the race.

To each person love differs according to his life-motive. In the last analysis there are two types of life-motive, those of the giver and the getter. Although *outwardly* both of these may express the same ideas, sentiments, ambitions and knowledge, this inner difference of motive causes them to vary profoundly in essence, in action, and in result.

For the giver is radiant, whereas the getter is magnetic.

Here is a vitally important psychological key which we should learn to understand and use. God is the great Giver. He spends a force and ingenuity which we cannot conceive on giving out this amazing world as we know it. Of what He gets we can have no idea, but we cannot deny the giving. Christ came to give us an example of selfless love. He gave all.

It is very difficult for us to understand selflessness. Our inhibitions prevent it. They include always the importance of the self and fear for the self, self-assertion and its inverted form—the inferiority complex.

Engrossment with the self is a necessary phase in the process of character-building, but it is only a phase. If the character does develop the next stage embraces the letting go of the self.

A self-centred person does, indeed, focus his whole attention on his own centre, his personality. Therefore he tries to draw everything *towards* himself and attach it to him. Thus his being becomes magnetic. Things and people are drawn to him, and into the radius of his attraction. But as he never reaches outwards to other centres than himself, he has obtained nothing to give to those who are drawn within his magnetic sphere. In order to obey the law of interaction, he must first take from them. This he does, literally feeding upon them, their life force, their ideas, their love. They may feel depleted, but the more that is drawn from them the stronger becomes the magnetic pull.

The getter builds up his life, his position, his ambition and his creative work from all which he sucks out of his immediate surroundings. Their weakening produces his store of false strength. He will give out to them in time from this store, and create the impression of being a generous and original person. But both he and those he influences are cut off by his self-centredness, because the focus of attention is no longer in the Creator, but in a fraction of the created, and they can therefore not draw upon universal wisdom and supply, but only upon a limited and particular fraction of it. Therefore barriers, restrictions, frustrations and deprivations are set up and a state of disharmony ensues.

A rather large percentage of people must obviously belong to the 'getter' class, because the world as a whole contains much disharmony, many barriers and much deprivation.

The life-motive of the 'giver' presents a quite different situation. His interest is focused *outside* himself and therefore his heart radiates outwards. His receptive channels are open to the universe, and so the universe flows into and through him. He receives abundantly, not because he desires all things for the self, but because he unites through his radiations with all things and becomes a part of all things. Through that unity he understands all things, and the love which he knows is the love which we must try to realise—it is compounded of union, understanding and radiation. It cannot be limited to one person because it flows constantly from, and to, and through everything.

The self is fulfilled and filled in this great stream and knows the unconsciousness of complete satisfaction. This unconsciousness naturally clears away all inhibitions and complexes because of course there is nothing to which they can attach themselves. If you are un-selfconscious you cannot have an inferiority complex or a personal fear. This, then, is the 'perfect freedom' which comes to the server of love, of selfless and universal love.

Such freedom is worth anything to obtain and to keep. We can hardly imagine a world in which everyone possessed such freedom and in which life was lived accordingly.

Let us continue the search within ourselves and discover whether in our hearts we belong to the givers or the getters. Until we can face this issue we can go no further along the road to fulfilment. If we will not face it we are holding fast the bolts of our own prison and of the prison of our race.

Many of us give in order to get—appreciation, a feeling of virtue or power, our own spiritual advancement. All this is *personal*, and it will really avail us nothing. A real giver gives because he cannot help it; he wants nothing except to aid, and the consequences (to himself) are of no interest to him. If everyone could give in this way where then would poverty, loneliness, hatred, and misery find a hold?

The least one of us, if we have this power of giving, be it in thought, word or deed, can be both free and powerful in the place and situation where we are. All inhibitions, all excuses, all compromises must fall to the ground before this truth. No one can bind our thoughts, which are more powerful and far-reaching than ourselves. No one can fetter our hearts, but through their radiations we can own and *be* the universe.

Let us cease to be engrossed with the restrictions set about our bodies and our brains, for they are the least part of us. Let us rather concentrate upon our true powers, and bend our endeavours and our understanding to the achieving of freedom—that freedom which is omnipotent: freedom from the self.

5

Our Double Natures

Some people are far more complex than others. They are usually the more intellectual, highly-developed and sensitive types. We can divide people fairly easily into three categories in this respect. Firstly, we have the people who are simple because they are primitive in character. Secondly, we have a large percentage of people who are complex because so many latent parts of them are developing in different directions and at different speeds. Thirdly, we have a small percentage of people who *have* developed most of their potentialities and achieved harmony between them. They have acquired the peace of fulfilment, and their very silence has an active and potent quality.

There are very few of these fulfilled people in our midst. We must therefore consign ourselves, as average people, to the second category, and assume that we have at least a double nature if not a more divided one.

Our immediate definition of a double nature would be that it is capable of both good and bad. It would therefore belong to one who was partly giver and partly getter, and whose life was thus founded upon a double motive.

Leading on from this simple division we will discover further and further complications within the human mind, both conscious and subconscious. In order to find our way we must try to form some idea of what the human mind actually is and where it functions. This, of course, is a subject which has perplexed the greatest sages throughout all time. All we can try to do in these pages is to find certain clues which will give us clarity as to our own mental complexes.

We must begin by emphasising the fact that the mind does not exist exclusively within the brain. The mind uses the brain but it exists all over the body, and can even leave it entirely and function apart from it. In the fingers of blind people the mind has sometimes focused to the extent of forming grey brain-matter there. There are also many cases of a patient under anaesthetic having watched the surgeon operating upon him from many feet above his own body.

We can really say that the whole body is actually the brain. I think that this is near to the truth and will make our subject clearer. The whole body is permeated by the mind. It is like a wireless set upon which are the receivers for a variety of wave-lengths. These receivers are the endocrine glands, or are secreted within them. There are seven major glands. The mind uses them as its instruments of thought and feeling and expression in various ways.

So we have the body with its head, spine, organs and glands, and we are looking upon it as the *large* brain of the mind.

Within the head is the brain with which we are more familiar, and which we will call the small brain. This brain is a very fair replica of the large body-brain, having much the form of a human embryo with rudimentary head, spine, organs and glands.*

So, just as you have the child, or replica, within the mother's womb, so you find the child-brain in the head and the larger brain of the body, which latter nourishes and develops it.

This is rather an unusual conception to make of the brain and mind, but it is one which is worth a thorough assimilation on our parts, because it is the true one. If we study the ancient sciences of the cosmic and spiritual laws, we will find that everything is a replica of something larger, with certain slight differences. The theme of the solar system is repeated from giant systems to lesser ones, right down to the solar system of the atom. Man's own solar system of heart and glands finds its place with all other living things within this pageant. So, also, we find the form of the embryo repeated in unexpected places, and herein lies much food for conjecture.

What is the explanation of this system of repetition?

We are told that it exists in order to weave and link the whole pattern of life together. It is the secret of the essential unity of the

* See *The Fifth Dimension*, Part I, Rider & Co.

universe. Could we but grasp this law, the unity of all life will become a fact for us. Astrology teaches it. We learn, for instance, that 'the sun rules the heart'. What does that mean?

It may mean that those radiations which are peculiar to the sun, other than the obvious ones of heat and light, are the ones which especially nourish, develop and determine the structure and functions of the heart—this being accomplished through similarity of vibration (of wave-length between the planet and the organ). The vibratory rate of the heart-tissue would be tuned as receiver to those particular sun radiations.

'The sun rules the heart'—not only the human heart but the heart of every living thing. It is the heart of the solar system.

The latest findings of science are interesting in this respect. The electrical wave-length of every organ in the body has been measured and listed. We are told that the wave-frequency of the human heart has been counted, and it has been found to coincide with that of the heart tissue of every living creature. The heart of a hen vibrates at the same rate as the heart of a king!

It is said to be the same with the liver—in all creatures the liver bears the same numbered wave-frequency. Astrology tells us that the liver in all creatures is ruled by the radiations peculiar to the planet Venus.

Where is all this leading us?

We must now consider a very significant point. Those same modern scientists declare that if we ascertain the *total* vibration or wave-length of a person we find that it is individual and unique to himself alone. Just as it is said to be the *total* vibration of Venus which is individual to that planet alone!

It appears that the individual vibration of every man is his unique possession—it can radiate round the world without becoming confused with the personal vibration of any of the other millions of living beings. A dog can scent it out, and it can cling to handkerchiefs or other personal belongings almost indefinitely.

We cannot dwell here upon this fascinating subject. We only touch upon it to help us with our study of the human mind and its individuality. In this connection we have made three points. Firstly, that the mind exists in every organ of the body, and in the gland which controls that organ. Secondly, that every organ and tissue in a body is linked by similarity of vibration to all its fellows in all living creatures. Thirdly, that in spite of this vast network of links between all life, each human individual carries a vibration unique to himself alone.

The existence of this unique vibration gives the lie to the more old-fashioned of the psychoanalysts, who left the individual soul out of their calculations, and who seemed to try to make out that man was but a set of automatic reflexes. Certain scientists have unexpectedly proved the existence of the individual soul or character; that a person's individuality can be measured in terms of vibrations; and that its influence can be traced around the globe.

Therefore we know that the mind itself is a link with all things, that each one of us possesses our own individuality, our own soul or motive-force which controls and uses mind within its radius; and does so through its interaction with life and matter through those linked channels, the organs, glands and their electrical centres or plexuses.

So we can picture man's link with the world as being through his larger brain, the body, and his link with his soul or individuality as being through his small brain in the head, and with the sun through his heart.

According to these assumptions we are now getting a most interesting light thrown on the subject of the glands. Authorities on spiritual science have always told us that the major endocrine glands, while controlling the major organs and activities of the body, are themselves controlled by that which lies at the heart of them—a little electrical plexus, known as a 'psychic centre' or 'chakra',* which acts as conductor or channel or link through which certain life forces, radiations and impressions flow. These psychic or electrical 'centres' have each their own wave-length which links them with certain cosmic building forces. These life forces shape and determine the chemical actions and nervous activities of the respective glands, who in their turn control the large organs such as the liver and heart.

Each large organ, therefore, is like a little nation or community of cells, its total vibration differing from the rest of the body, and being under a physical government (the gland) whose real individuality and life-force lies within its psychic centre. It is not very difficult to picture this arrangement. Whereas the ancient

* Indian name for these centres of force.

scientists knew much about the psychic centres, modern scientists have determined a great deal about the action of the glands on the human organism and character.

In fact they have almost given us the impression that a man is the slave of his glands, and that his mind and character are dependent upon them. This is a puzzling doctrine for a 'Christian' public to accept, who are supposed to believe in 'free-will'. We must, however, remember the fallibility of specialists, who often cannot see the wood for the trees—or even for their particular leaf!

We who are trying to look at the matter broadly, have visioned the mind as permeating the whole body and as using the glands and centres as parts of this 'larger brain'. Therefore we are able to declare that it is the mind which can influence the glands in the first place. We can see how a strong inhibition set up in childhood could, and most certainly *would*, influence not only the whole body, but especially that particular gland and centre in the body which had some relation to it. The glands must form a framework of focal points which represent the component parts of the mind and express their respective degrees of development.

In the last analysis, the ultimate organisation of these glands lies in a fine network of nerve systems and channels, through which the 'electric' forces tapped by the centres circulate. Therefore it comes down to this : that our whole beings, from both the mental and physical angle, are worked by electricity. We are, of course, using the word 'electricity' loosely, to cover a vast assortment of radiations of which our common electricity is but one.

The actual functioning and building up of both mind and physique is therefore motivated and worked by the *same* substances—those forces and activities which include light, heat and radiation.

If we can realise this, we can quite easily see that the same forces which are flowing through a certain centre to build a certain thought-form or impression, must and do affect the chemical activities in their neighbourhood and therefore the organic tissue which is being formed.

If the mind is undisciplined and uncontrolled, or in other words *not* governed by a strong life-motive, it is not itself in control of its larger brain and the glands and centres. Therefore a habit which is set up in any of them is allowed to grow and accumulate magnetism, until it definitely affects and influences the mind. We then say that a man is the slave of his glands. But that is the end of the story—the beginning lay in his own original lack of ideals and of wilful life-motive.

Remember that we are discussing in this book the *average* man in his millions. There would be no point in bringing up in this argument the rare pathological cases in which people are born with very abnormal glands. These instances have served to emphasise and teach the functions and powers of the glands, but in studying them we must always remember that they are the exceptions which prove our rule.

The gland specialists tell us, however, that even average and normal people are all 'glandular types'—that is to say, that the influence of one particular gland always predominates, even in a balanced character, and determines our general type and reactions. It will be helpful if we take a brief survey of these findings of science, and we can then use them in our process of self-analysis. For this purpose we will briefly recapitulate what we said in a former book.*

The principal endocrine glands are, as we know, the pituitary in the front of the brain, the pineal in the middle of the head, the thyroid and parathyroids in the throat, the thymus in the chest, the pancreas in the region of the solar plexus, the adrenals just above the kidneys, and the gonads in the groins.

Each of these glands manufactures one or more subtle secretions which pass into the blood stream and do their specialised work. These glands act as brakes or controls upon each other, and a system of balanced interaction between them produces the perfect human being. Under-action, over-action, or disease in any one of them upsets this system and results in a variety of symptoms and abnormalities.

One of these glands is always in major control of the system. From babyhood to adulthood they take over the control in successive phases, finally to produce the completed human being. After that their arrangement will depend upon the individual development of their owner.

The thymus is the first gland to take control of the human being. It builds the child, and all that pertains to the child. Its sovereignty lasts until the arrival of a permanent set of teeth,

* See *The Initiation of The World*, Rider & Co.

after which it should retire into the background, giving way to the dominance of the thyroid. If, unfortunately, the thymus continues in control, the growing person remains permanently childish, with a babyish skin, a weak will and irresponsible tendencies.

The 'centre' in the region of the thymus is, of course, the heart centre. This is the channel through which impersonal universal love radiates outwards and links with that quick wordless intuitive knowledge which is the real wisdom. This centre is active in childhood, which is why Christ said :

'Except ye become as little children ye shall in no wise enter into the kingdom of heaven.'

By the end of childhood, environment has crushed and inhibited and repressed the response to this centre, which becomes inactive at the recession of the thymus, and remains but a latent power, possible of revival in later life, under the stimulus of matured ideality.

The thyroid gland comes into dominance at about the eighth year. Its work is the production of energy. It gives the child that vitality, magnetism, and impulsive, explosive quality which carries on his development to adolescence. At this age the thyroid sovereignty should cease, but if it does not do so, as sometimes in the case of singers who are constantly stimulating it, we see a continuation of excitement, brain-storms and temper all through life.

At adolescence the adrenal glands should take over the rulership. They release large reserves of extra energy which develop mentality, sex characteristics, ambition, quick reaction to fright and the fighting instinct, and extreme emotional activity. At maturity the gonads, or sex glands have come into full play, and round off the human being completely, producing in normal development altruism, warmheartedness and a sense of protectiveness. We are familiar with the under-sexed or over-sexed types, and they do not concern us here.

The pituitary should come into dominance at a later phase in human development, at about the age of forty-nine. This is when man should really reach his prime, and his matured intellect should begin to assert itself. In a distressingly large percentage of cases this never happens at all !

The pituitary controls two phases of intellectual development,

that of practical intellectuality and that of sentiment. It can produce the mathematician, the poet, or the two combined. It is the
medium for creative and abstract thought, the receptor of
inspiration. The whole of the life should be building up towards
the dominance of the pituitary, which should give it its final
flowering and expression.

The pineal is the real secret ruler of the human system, working subtly to inaugurate the functions of the glands, and to control the action of light upon the body. It is made of the same
tissue as are the eyes. It was once a third eye, able to discern
radiations and non-solid forms. Its powers are supposed to be
atrophied, but they are only latent and misunderstood. Spiritual
scientists declare that the 'centre' in the region of the pineal is
the channel through which the 'I', the individual soul, links with
spiritual knowledge. This channel can be linked to the intellect
if the radiations or auras of the pineal and pituitary can meet.
This is the aim of yogis and of sages, but it can come about naturally, through the *single-motive* of an utter will to good.

'If thine eye be single, thy whole body shall be full of light.'

This refers, as we have said, to the purity of motive which will
awaken the true function of the pineal gland, the eye of the
spirit, which will enlighten the whole body, the larger mind.

The pineal can act as a check on sex activity. The pituitary is
made of the same tissue as the thyroid in the throat and works
with it, through speech, to achieve creative expression.

Each gland has many more activities than those we have mentioned. The variety of types caused by the varied balancing up
and development of the glands is as numerous as the population
of the world—for in everyone it is different. An expert can add
up the sum of a person's glandular development by looking at
him. Hair, eyes, teeth, bones, movements, all are signposts of
glandular activities.

The gland specialist will leave it at that. But we, who have
declared that in the last analysis it is the mind working within
the glands which determines all things, will be able gradually to
work out causes and results from this angle.

The scientists cure extreme cases of glandular abnormality
through operations, electrical and radiatory stimulation, mas-
sage and biochemistry. In many cases a psychological basis for
the defect is recognised and psychological or mental treatment is

given too. In the latter instance, the understanding and co-operation and will-power of the patient is usually necessary to effect a cure, but in bad cases it is often impossible to achieve this.

We are not, however, considering extreme pathological cases, but far subtler ones which probably never come into the doctor's hands, those of the average man and woman. Their personalities are made up of certain little habits of thought and action, due to their particular glandular-mental make-up. You and I can be our own physicians in this matter when once we realise that in nine cases out of ten any symptoms and peculiarities we may possess are due *not* to some obscure, complex physical condition, which we could not hope to understand or treat, but to a habit of thought which lies behind and creates that condition, and with which only we can come to grips.

If we allow ourselves to concentrate unduly on the gratification of any organ of the body our mind-power centres in it, our nourishing blood cells congregate there. The organ acquires more than its share of magnetism and importance and a power-complex grows within it. The little community of cells becomes an autarchy and dreams of world domination. Imperative cravings are set up, and the human being, because of his initial slackness in control, finds himself faced with a tyrant within his own body. The tyrant may take the form of physical craving for drugs, drink or sex, or of mental craving for excitement, power, amusement or idleness. There is bound to be, as we have seen, great interplay between physical and mental symptoms. Once this condition of tyranny is set up the victim may neither appreciate its seriousness, know how to deal with it, nor have the will-power to do so.

How did this unfortunate condition actually arise?

Firstly, there was the lack of a high and clear life-motive. The wish to achieve any fine goal in living causes the preservation of health and bodily control and balance to become an automatic practice. This is achieved in accordance with the strength and purity of the motive. Therefore, to start a child off in life with a high personal ambition for integrity and service would be the best insurance you could give him against becoming the prey of bad habits or abnormalities in his glandular or personal make-up. Only a strong individual belief, or ambition, or ideal will produce will-power sufficient to carry its owner ahead past all side issues and temptations. Even if the ambition be evil, the will-power will serve it if the motive be strong enough.

All things serve singleness of motive. If we can imbue the weakest, most inefficient and ineffectual character with a simple conviction and the will to act accordingly, a miraculous transformation will follow. By the same token we often find a person, brilliant, accomplished and attractive in all his parts, who yet achieves nothing at all because motive and will are missing, or are intermittent.

Once again the challenge is the same. If we are troubled and hampered by a 'double nature', changeableness, cravings or habits, do not let us blame them for our inefficiency. Our best method will be to ignore and forget them by degrees by building up an inspiring motive for our lives. Let us dwell on the exciting, stimulating and fascinating aspects of this life-motive. Thus we will gradually draw away all the wrongly concentrated powers of our mind, our blood and our subtler forces and direct them to nobler issues.

We can best 'kill out' our unfortunate tendencies by an effortless neglect of them. If we have intelligence and determination we shall find the way, especially if we remember that the key to that way always lies in letting go of the self.

6

Are We Logical?

We have seen that the whole question as to what we do with our lives depends upon the motive, conscious or subconscious, for which we live. To determine such a motive requires in the first place a little thinking, however simple. The mind is the link between the will of the 'I' and the actions of the body and brain. Therefore, whatever the 'I' desires it must influence and train the mind to accomplish.

The will is the engine driver, the mind is the engine, and the heart is the power, the fuel, the heat which ultimately makes the whole thing go.

Accordingly, we are effective if our will, mind and heart work *together*. This is the goal before us. People readily admit that their hearts 'run away with them', or that their emotions 'get the better of them', or that they are 'beside themselves with rage', or that they are the 'prey of their imaginations'. Sometimes they suffer all these things by turns. Others, in fear of part of their own selves, choose to rely on their brains, on 'common sense'. They wish to rely on the engine without putting any fuel in it. They become lifeless people who shun experience.

All these are examples of glandular unbalance, because the work is not being equally shared out between those living centres in the body which control the glands, the centres of heart, brain and will. In a properly balanced man of will-power the will streams from the brain-centre, and the power streams from the heart-centre. People in a position of power endure great strain on their hearts. Big business bosses often drop dead from heart failure at some quite mild exercise, such as golf, which in ignorance they have added to an already overworked heart. The heart centre is not a reservoir of power. It is a channel through which power flows, like electric currents, on the cosmic rays.

The individual works the switch which controls this current, and can keep it turned on or off. When the current is on he can direct it for use through his mind centre, or let it run wild, in which case it over-stimulates the emotions.

Have you ever thought of the enormous and inexhaustible power tapped by a little human being? A well-conditioned man can run a score of miles without apparently using up anything! His little body could not contain the cans of petrol, hundred-weights of coal, or heavy electric batteries, that would be required to make a small engine perform the same feat.

In many other ways man has access to an enormous amount of power. The mind even acts as a strong brake upon this power. We know this, because under hypnosis a human being can put forth many times his normal strength without apparent effort or ill effects. It is important for us to realise that we all have access to a formidable current of power which can be converted to various uses, muscular and mental.

In singleness of motive the whole of this power is directed to one end. In mixed motives the power is split up and often divided against itself. Therefore, from yet another angle, the importance logically of following one clear life motive is made plain.

We now come to the question as to what degree the average human being is logical? What do we infer by this word? I think we mean by 'logic' the capacity to face the fact that certain actions or causes produce inevitable results, and to act upon this knowledge.

Most of us do no such thing. Firstly, we usually do not seek to face this uncomfortable mathematical table of cause and result. Secondly, we often prefer to ignore what is brought quite plainly to our notice, and continue to live illogically, hoping for the best. Most people really know that late nights, lack of sleep, overfeeding, wrong diet, and artificial stimulants, both mental and physical, provide the surest methods of slow and painful suicide. Yet they continue to apply this method, failing to observe that they and their companions reach the grave on an average of some thirty to sixty years sooner than they should do. If they are forced to see a doctor they dislike him if he tells them the truth. Illogic rules our lives in their simplest terms at the present time.

'Oh, but *I* am not like that,' you say. 'I live a decent, restrained, regular life. I've no bad habits. I pride myself on my common sense—or logic, as you call it !'

Let us see.

Presumably we take an interest in everyday affairs. Very likely we criticise the actions of various authorities, the words of certain M.P.s, the attitude of the Government. We may even bitterly upbraid them all.

Yet we have been given the vote. We have our own representative in Parliament. What are we doing about that? Do we take an interest, a permanent interest, in him, his ideas and his works? Does he know what we want and what we think? Do we through him contribute our fair share of thought and of ambition for our own successful governing? Doubtless we believe in government for the people by the people, but without fulfilling our own obligations in this respect.

It is surely the height of illogic to sit in an armchair and criticise our democratic government if we do not fulfil our parts as democrats and do our share. We may excuse ourselves with the plea that our M.P. is abroad and we have no means of obtaining a hearing in our constituency.

Nevertheless, we always have the Press. Many newspapers owe much of their popularity to the fact that they allow expression to the views of their readers.

'Ahem ! I had a letter in *The Times* today....'

Also the Press is bound to keep its finger on the pulse of public opinion. If our views are strong and keen enough we will obtain a hearing. Moreover, the Press embraces an enormous range and variety of publications. That which one paper may not publish another will.

We should therefore be sufficiently logical to back up our own views, always assuming that we have had the wits to determine them. If we can do neither then it is illogical of us to open our mouths on the subject in question.

The same argument applies to our attitude to the Church. It is surely illogical of us to complain of the failure of the Church to satisfy our needs unless we have clearly emphasised to the Church what these needs are, and unless we have in some small measure contributed thought and study to what is admittedly considered to be so vitally important a subject.

The Church is drawn from our own ranks to fill our own needs. She is therefore but one more expression of ourselves. If we blame her, as an entity apart from ourselves, for failure, we are illogical and, moreover, stand self-accused.

As regards the Commandments of the Christian faith, have we ever faced them, and measured them against the living conditions that our governments have allotted to us?

'Thou shalt not kill.'

Does that mean that we should not go to war? Or that, if we put ourselves into the position that we *have* to go to war, it is an unfortunately unavoidable crime? If this is so, why have Christian nations glorified war instead of apologising for it?

If war is a crime then the things that lead up to war are criminal—unfairness, lack of give and take, power-lust, quarrelsomeness, greed—everything, in fact, which is contrary to the injunction to love our neighbours as ourselves. There are a thousand ways, in business and in other spheres, in which we can help or hinder other nations than our own. Do we ever try to find out what they are? Christ explained to us that the thought which led up to a crime was as bad as the crime. Therefore the attitudes which lead to war are criminal.

'Thou shalt not kill.'

Other fine religions have taken this literally and refused to feed upon the flesh of helpless animals. Their population and health seem in no way to have declined.

Where do we stand on this important point? Christ did not scorn the carpenter's bench, but we cannot imagine Him assisting in a slaughter-house. He said : 'Inasmuch as ye have done it unto the least of these my brethren, ye have done it unto me.' If we condemn thousands of our fellow-men to a life of slaughtering we are thus also condemning Him.

Many of us love animals and yet we eat them. And we use them mercilessly. Several people have spent a lifetime making known to the public the horrible cruelties which take place in the procuring of furs. Yet there has been no horrified outcry on the part of the public, merely a slightly resentful silence. Fur coats are beautifully warm and make us look so well dressed ! Surely it is not our affair how they are procured—we would rather not think about it !

Yet if we ask the average person whether he honestly considers it right or wrong to be cruel to animals—faced with this plain issue and not allowed to prevaricate—he will undoubtedly say that it is very wrong. Nevertheless, he will almost certainly argue and hedge when definite cases of cruelty, such as blood-sports, fur-trapping, vivisection, caging and so on, are brought up for his condemnation. I have even heard an apparently intelligent person declare that the fox likes to be hunted! Such an attitude is death to progress and to honesty. It is indeed incomprehensible. We can never acquire straight and successful minds if we wriggle round subjects in this way.

You and I will agree at once, I feel sure, that people should be as consistently kind and protective to animals as lies in their power. Then let us be logical right through in our attitude to this question and begin by admitting that we impose upon animals in every way for our own convenience. Once we establish the *will* to alter all this the means will come to hand.

I believe that so long as men oppress, restrict, imprison, torture and slaughter animals, they will do the same to each other. They so saturate their own auras with the effluvia of cruelty, fear and suffering that they become befogged and can no longer see anything in a reasonable light. Animals are much nearer to men than the latter realise. Many believe that the animal soul is as vital as man's, but is evolving along different lines, and for a different purpose. To eat animals closely resembles cannibalism. It is also a very extravagant method of feeding, and one which breeds many diseases.

From the psychological angle, the animal nature and the animal mind are as firmly rooted in its glands and organs as are our own. It is recognised that average meat-eaters are prone to passion, to pugnaciousness, to quarrelsomeness, and to the persistent craving for more food and stimulants. This is quite natural, for meat is not a food but a stimulant, and it creates a vicious circle of craving within the body. It often necessitates a heavy and varied diet, or other sedatives or stimulants to supplement it.

The whole question of flesh-eating has been argued back and forth. Everything said against it has been well substantiated. In any case, the horrible prevalence of a variety of monstrous diseases, such as cancer, tuberculosis, and rheumatism in its many phases, should be sufficient answer in itself to our way of feeding.

Yet people continue to believe what they wish to believe. They compromise with their own habits and desires and continue to live suicidally and illogically.

This will not do for us. Our process of self-analysis cuts right through it. We have clearly to face this issue of cruelty to animals in its various forms. For we cannot build up a life in which we 'love our neighbour' in the complete sense, while yet we act in a diametrically opposite way with our other beautiful living neighbours, the animals. Only dire inner confusion and hypocrisy, so deep-seated that we have lost the sense of it, results from this compromise, and double motives sap as usual our best powers.

Those groups who work against cruelty to animals in all its forms are labelled by some of us as 'cranks'. Admittedly certain of them sometimes exceed a normal zeal, much as we may do over golf or bridge, or other amusements of a non-altruistic type. But at least they have the honour of attempting something worth while, and if it was not such uphill work they probably would keep quite balanced !

Most humanitarian groups, working a generation or so ahead of their time, were known as cranks, or worse, and doubtless contained a few cranks within their ranks. We would be ashamed now to contemplate the abuses which they were able to have abolished in the teeth of much opposition.

If we are sincere we will not be put off by considerations of the type of people who subscribe to certain ideas, or the jokes that are made about them. We will only consider the ideas themselves, in their personal application to ourselves and our own concerns.

Do *we* condemn cruelty to animals, either by overworking them, or by caging them in solitary confinement, or by inflicting prolonged agony on them in procuring their pelts, or by vivisecting and experimenting upon them in a variety of cruel ways in the 'interests' of science?

Do we condemn all this? Or do we turn a deaf ear and a blind eye to it all, and go along stolidly profiting by the results?

'Oh, but, come !' you say. 'What about the enormous saving of life and immunity from disease accomplished through inoculations, vaccinations, etc. ?'

There again we open up a tremendous field for arguing back and forth. What a pathetic situation ! After having subjected our bodies to disease, by flesh-eating, wrong diet and habits, and poisonous mental activities, we turn once more to the animals and fill ourselves with noxious and often beastly serums which are frequently impregnated with the effluvia of their agony and terror. (And even if this is not always true we do not trouble to find out.) It is indeed a vicious circle. For, although we may at the time apparently cure or prevent a disease which should never have threatened, we shall be condemned ourselves to worse or more prolonged disease in the future by thus contaminating our blood stream. In fact, such a disease as cancer is strongly suspect in this connection.

For those who wish to study this question many statistics have been compiled and much research upon these subjects has been written up.

Why, however, should we wade through all this? However convincing, would it convince us?

'A man convinced against his will is of the same opinion still!' What is our *will*?—that is the point.

If our own will is against cruelty to animals we do not need arguments. We simply know that Christ or any Christ-like man or woman would say that there is no possible excuse for any kind of cruelty to or imposition on animals—'the least of these my brethren'—and that if our spiritual sense of honour is really alive we would prefer to die than to live at their expense.

Although we have misused science in many ways, she is always ready to serve us in those matters by producing the tangible answer to our questions. Just now we are forced, because of world economics, to study the problems of home produce on our islands. The exigencies of the situation are impelling the admission that a comparatively fleshless diet in this country would be far more economical, healthier and better from the point of view of employment and distribution of the population.

There are those who hold back from this admission on the grounds that our foggy and heavy climate makes a quick stimulant like meat necessary. They ignore the fact that in a correctly understood fleshless diet there is a richer quantity of alcoholic or sugar stimulant of a type whose effect is far more durable than that of meat. Such a diet is infinitely less extravagant from the point of view of national economy and more independent from the point of view of home production. It is also more humanising, as it removes thousands from the ghastly occupations of slaughter and butchery, and places them to healthy and sweet work with the living fruits of the earth.

Let us not trouble with arguments and statistics over this issue, but rather accept the simple principle that as it is the better and more spiritual way it must therefore be the wiser and more practical way, too.

'But what is going to happen to the animals if we cease to need them—will they all have to be destroyed?'

If we have studied the activities and functions of animal life only a little* we will have an answer ready for this. The economy of nature is built on a system of exchange, of give and take, in which animals play an essential part. They produce chemical changes in the atmosphere and in vegetable life. They are a link in the chain of growth and evolution which cannot be broken without the collapse of the whole system. The animals feed upon superfluous greenstuff and keep the earth manured and fertile. We could find ways of determining their numbers without callousness or cruelty. We could continue to clothe ourselves most luxuriously with their combings and clippings, without such wholesale use of the complete hide. We could continue to enjoy that intimacy with animals which brings a unique ecstasy into human living.

Once the *motive* of fairness and consideration to animals is established in our minds, situations will change accordingly, so that its practice becomes possible. Unseen forces are always waiting to bring about that for which we wish. The world is fashioned by the motives of men. If we can once possess ourselves of a clear and uncompromising decision not to tyrannise over animals, things which we now look upon as necessary will become impossible. It would be impossible nowadays, for instance, to send a little child down to work in a mine, yet not so long ago this was considered entirely necessary—for economic reasons!

It is only necessary to realise that if we do believe in an intelligent God, Who must perforce also be a logical One, then the more logically we think and live the nearer we will approximate to Divine conception.

We have only touched upon a few, a very few, of our illogicalities here, but more will spring to the mind as we think of them.

* See *The Initiation of The World,* Rider & Co.

We will be able to trace the same two-sided attitude, double motives, and compromise in our relationship to everything we do, and in our reactions to everything that happens to us. As a result, our lives and those of the community in which we live are fashioned like a kaleidoscope of disconnected pieces, welded into a whole by force of circumstances and blind seeking to serve our own interests. And yet the simple change to serving our neighbours' interests instead would reverse the kaleidoscope into an ordered and beautiful design.

7

The Reckoning

If we can accept the fact that chaotic thinking makes for chaotic living conditions we will agree that to change our mode of thought would be the surest way to produce changes in our environment and activities. Many feel that new laws and innovations must arrive before new ways of thinking and acting become possible. But no innovations stand much chance either of being promoted or successfully carried through without a certain measure of the people's will and of their support.

There are always a number of powerful individuals who, from self interest, feel compelled to block the way to any progressive changes. Only the will of the majority of the public can prevail against such obstructions. Therefore the true beginnings of all progress rest with such as you and myself. It is our steady wishes, flowing continually through the ethers, which inspire the pioneers who are sensitive to the trends of thought and evolution, and who translate human hopes and desires into terms of planning and invention.

It is thus true that whatsoever we intelligently and sincerely wish for we shall obtain. 'Ask and ye shall receive' is a *natural* law when properly applied.

In order to get our wish and our will clarified it is quite necessary that we clearly see the situation as it actually is at present, both in respect of ourselves and in respect of the community. Our reasonings in these chapters should have taken us some way towards this goal by now.

Presumably we are agreed that the world is at present in an appalling state of chaos which has gradually reached its climax in the current period of history. Men of religion, of politics and of letters are all admitting it to us. We can define this situation in our minds by remembering a variety of accepted facts.

For instance, there is the fact that after many centuries of so-called civilised development we are forced to spend all our resources of time, money and strength in the occupation of killing each other and destroying our mutual possessions, or threatening to do so!

It is true, also, that in a world where there is space and labour and goods for everyone, many are devoid of everything, while wastage, destruction of the fruits of the earth, extravagance and inequality abound.

Moreover, it seems that our Church dare not and cannot uphold its own laws and principles, and has to exist in a state of compromise.

Also, although there are constant superficial improvements, the actual state of public health is appalling. Many diseases flourish, of which only one, cancer, kills about 110,000 annually in England and Wales. And, besides the more obvious diseases, we are all very far from what we could and should be in general health and longevity.

Furthermore, education itself equips us with no real ideals, ambitions, or competence to reach our highest potentialities. Even if it did so the unnatural spectre of unemployment is always there to undermine our confidence.

Finally, we are faced with the possibility that at any moment war may lead to annihilation and disintegration throughout our civilised world, and that we have as yet no guarantee that further wars may not extinguish us altogether.

We must lastly acknowledge the fact that this state of affairs is the direct result of the collective intelligence, wishes and interests of the community, which community includes you and me, and our parents and grandparents. (We have each of us been moulded by the influence of sixteen great-great-grandparents.)

A further difficulty lies in the fact that even if we, the people, acknowledge and accept these deplorable truths we usually feel totally inadequate either clearly to perceive how the necessary changes should be brought about, or how to insist upon them if we do.

Is it really true that we are and must remain so ineffectual? We seem able to do little else than criticise the government and any others who wield power, blaming them for our unhappy state. Nevertheless, if it has been rightly said that a people has the government it deserves, the task before us is to find out what changes we must individually make in order to deserve that for which we wish—or ought to wish !

If the fault does indeed largely lie with the individual then let us not hold up better times indefinitely, but get down to the essentials now and quickly.

One of the truths we must realise is that most of us have not the courage to love. I refer, of course, to that impersonal love which we have already defined. Fettered by fear for ourselves and our personal possessions and responsibilities, we simply dare not share our efforts and our care for the good of all.

This lack of love is really against nature. It starts a vicious circle. It is actually an inhibition caused by a variety of fears. It inhibits or prevents us properly from perceiving and contemplating—and therefore understanding—the subject in question. Love is an unrestricted unification, both spiritually and mentally, through the heart, with the object of its regard. It therefore brings the completest understanding of that object's qualities, difficulties, function and potentialities. If love could take its true place as the natural involuntary function of the heart, the people would have a one-pointed desire for that which was best and fairest for all. Personal considerations could not hamper their judgement. The world would become a fair place because they would, of course, obtain the government which they had come to desire and deserve.

This may all sound so simple as to be unworthy of consideration. Nevertheless, it does constitute the essential truth which we are up against. There is no other way. It must be a part, and the fundamental part, of any progressive changes which are brought about, if they are to ensure the people's happiness. We can each contribute our share individually, by self-analysis and self-culture along the lines we are indicating, and by spreading the ideal in schools, in the literary and dramatic worlds, and in all spheres which deal with propaganda and education.

We must never forget the importance of the individual and the tremendous influence he may wield once he is fired by an ideal. It may be that we excuse ourselves from this implication on various grounds. Perhaps we are so busy and so tired making ends

meet that we feel any further effort is impossible. Just as a tuber-
cular person might say he was too weak to take a few extra steps
into the sunshine to get cured. Or we may be cruelly handicapped
by some physical or mental disability, some hereditary affliction,
which we feel should fairly excuse us from all pioneering efforts.

If this be so, we should remember that very many of our
greatest geniuses and benefactors, musicians, orators, fighters,
have suffered from the severest handicaps, such as epilepsy,
blindness, deafness, stuttering, or chronic ill-health. Indeed, the
psychoanalyst, Adler, originated his Theory of Compensation
with reference to these cases. He suggested that a severe affliction
of sòme kind often challenges its victim, stimulating him into
such supreme efforts to overcome it that a brilliant achievement
is the result.

Therefore the argument that there are handicaps which are
sufficient to prevent us from playing our fair part in human
evolution must fall at once to the ground in face of historical
testimony. Beethoven was deaf, Milton was blind, Napoleon was
an epileptic—so was the great reformer Tutankhamen, while the
number of orators who have begun life with a bad defect in
speech is legion.

On the other hand, we may seek refuge from effort with the
plea that we are too simple-minded, uneducated, and ordinary.
Yet what about Joan of Arc, the village maid? What about
scores of leaders and reformers who have sprung from 'the
gutter', or of simple peasant visionaries who have inspired hundreds? There is no limit to what any one of us might do if we
once learnt to put ourselves in singleness of motive at the service
of our Creator through a loving understanding of His works.

Either we must one day make this effort, all of us, or we must
continue to live in fear, drudgery, apathy, ill-health, and ignorance, and in an environment of slums, war, and insecurity. That
is our punishment for our lack of interest in our own fate, and
even if these things do not seem outwardly to be affecting our
lives, they are affecting us very powerfully from the sphere of
radiations. But we have grown too accustomed to this heavy
punishment. We accept it all as the natural course of events, and
so continue to turn our backs upon the joyous life which could
be ours.

If we could only dare to *love,* and to go forward into under-

standing we should begin to live a new life in a new world. Our
forces would be multiplied because our lives would cease to be
filled with incessant waste of energy over things that do not
matter. Our needs would decrease, partly because of a growing
simplification in our living, and partly because of our conserved
force. Quantities of tonics, stimulants, superficial entertainment,
and medical attention would become unwanted. The happiness
of our new way of life would spread like an epidemic, and many
would gain the courage to embrace it.

Our new way of life with its singleness of purpose and of vision
would strengthen our intuition. We would know whom to trust
and whom to follow. The next generation would be profoundly
affected, and the hero-worship which is a natural instinct of
youth would find a reasonable and satisfying outlet in emulating
our own efforts. That which we were accomplishing with difficulty would be far more easily acquired by the young and
become their natural tendency.

As for ourselves, we would have found freedom, escape—from
conditioning—and a fulfilment undreamt of by those who re-
mained encrusted in their shells of inhibition. Order would come
into our lives, a rightful flow of all things back and forth. The
fetish of family life would not encumber us. We would realise
that only a fourth of our capacity for service was due to the family
(or our personal affairs), and that we owe as much allegiance to
our community, to our nation and to our world.

Here is a fact and a responsibility which it is essential that we
should grasp with all its implications. It is not enough to love,
enjoy and serve those of our own family. The chaos and slaughter
in the world today is produced by people who in the main live
devoted family lives. It is better if we enter also into the life of
the community, sharing its cares and responsibilities and helping
where we can. But this is not enough either. It has not prevented
mass hypnotism, unemployment, exploitation, slums, ignorance
and other evils which still hold the community in thrall.

It is better if we try to enter into the problems of our country,
helping all we can in the governing of ourselves and the perfect-
ing of those attributes which will develop us into a fine, accomplished and successful nation. If we live thus, with our allegiance
equally divided between family, community and nation, we shall
be a tower of strength to all who know us.

But it will not be enough ! There are many such in many countries, but that has not prevented us from being threatened with world-wide extinction. It has, on the contrary, largely helped to inflate that perverted patriotism which holds national sovereignty in force, and whose motto is : 'My country and its interests first, at the expense of all else !'

No, it is only when an interest and a loyalty to the family of nations as a whole grips us that we can develop a truly constructive attitude, and give service that will be successful because founded upon true vision.

Men are taking an extraordinarily long time to realise this very simple truth. They cling in terror to their old restrictions, distrusts and complications, although they are being ruined by them. They can trust neither themselves, each other, or even God. A beauteous, generous world of plenty lies around them, all for them, and they simply do not seem able to believe it. They allow their lives to be directed and misdirected, without understanding that they should and could exert their own influence in the matter. The only way in which this can be accomplished is by cultivating the broadest vision possible and fitting problems into such a setting, that instead of the cramped and shortsighted vision which they are usually accorded, they are seen in the light of that universal aspect which even the tiniest problem actually has.

Therefore the man who can share out his allegiance, his interest, his vision and his service equally between his home, his community, his nation and his world, is the man who will really achieve something of true value to his God and to his fellow-men —and it is this for which subconsciously most men are craving.

8

Personal Armageddon

There are many people who go through a private and personal Armageddon of their own without even their nearest and dearest suspecting it at all.

They are ravaged at times by a terrible feeling of frustration or unfulfilment, although they may apparently have enjoyed all that life has to offer, in respect of family, of home and of career. They feel lonely, they feel restless, they feel nervous and irritable, without apparent reason. These feelings may become so strong that they darken and destroy all their happiness, and at times are well-nigh unbearable.

This private hell takes many forms, some easily recognisable and others vague and subtle. The victim may refuse to submit to these moods, and go firmly and cheerfully through his days, obstinately ignoring the danger signals from his innermost being. Finally, everyone is surprised when he has a sudden nervous breakdown, commits suicide, goes out of his mind, or revolts in some other way against the routine of his life.

'Such a successful man!' people exclaim. 'The last person one would have expected that to happen to!'

Usually the victim himself has not realised his own predicament, because for one thing he has not faced himself in order to find out the cause of his subtle trouble, and secondly he has not possessed the requisite knowledge with which successfully to perform such a psychoanalysis. Furthermore, in many cases, if he should for a moment suspect the true cause of his sufferings, that would be sufficient to make him evade the issue with determination, and obstinately pretend to himself that nothing was the matter. He can only mark time, however, for this inner affliction which has fastened upon him will never be gainsaid. The fight is on, and if he persists in ignoring this crisis within himself he will cause a short-circuit in his own being, and his life, although outwardly much the same, inwardly will be broken. He will become either a shell, automatically continuing his career although his real life urge has gone, or an eccentric or fanatic who is continually seeking escape in some hobby or excitement with which he dopes himself; or actually a drink, drug or sex addict, although his life may have been blameless hitherto; or a potential mental case, a melancholic, or a suicide.

Such a crisis in a person's life usually builds up around middle age, although it may take place at any age. If it is brought to the notice of the average psychoanalyst he will usually not be able to deal with it. But we are on the eve of a new type of psychoanalysis, which points to being successful in just such cases. This is because it takes into account a factor left out and ignored by the earlier schools of this science—the factor of the human soul.

The earlier psychoanalysts were 'materialists' to the degree that they tried to ascribe all human reactions to 'automatic reflexes', hereditary, atavism, race memory, and so on. Whereas these things did indeed account for a number of phenomena, they left an equal number completely unexplained and led to any amount of confused verbiage and theory.

The latest exponents of psychoanalysis have begun to understand that in view of the fact that the human soul has been accepted, explained, trained and held in high regard by cultured men throughout history, it might possibly actually exist, and if so would undoubtedly have some kind of effect upon the body, mind and personality whom it informed.

It seems strange that it should have been such a daring innovation for physicians and psychologists to begin taking the human soul into account in their studies of the human being. But so it was, and to this day most of these learned men would hesitate to use the word 'soul' to any of their patients.

Yet at all events the psychoanalysts have been gradually forced to take issue with this subject. A few of the more advanced have actually begun to try to psychoanalyse the soul. As members of any religion, our chief concern would appear to be, ostensibly, with our souls; so that to seek to know a little about them ought not to appear too outlandish. Furthermore, the Bible makes a very marked distinction between the soul and the spirit, so we evidently should be clear about that also.

In order to summarise such a big subject for our present purpose we might state that when talking of Spirit we refer to that great urge to manifest and to progress which is behind all life, and which is the living purpose of the Creator—that which is the great life-consciousness, the Great 'I'. This Spirit, in order to affect and work in the visible world, must individualise, or become clothed in individual characteristics, whether of animal, plant or man. Such a unit of individualisation is a lesser 'I', part of the great 'I' which has lost its sense of the whole for the time being, through its imprisonment within a living creature. We often hear the phrase 'All is spirit.' If that is so, what is the difference between the spirit which manifests as flesh and the spirit which controls or inhabits that flesh? It has been said that the latter is in a state of higher advancement, and is inhabiting the former for the purpose of teaching it, enlightening it and transmuting it to its own higher stage of progress. Could this suddenly occur, the flesh would disappear and all would be spirit!

If we first consider the *person of flesh,* we have begun to understand that he is an aggregate of cells arranged in communities, each controlled and ensouled by its own entity or intelligence. Therefore that which we know as the 'lower man' or 'man's lower nature' refers to this community of living intelligences who are running his machine for him. His job is to learn to control them and keep them in a state of right 'balance of power'.

If one of these intelligences becomes quite out of hand and achieves abnormal development, we say that the man is obsessed by an evil genius—but we do not cognise that this evil genius is an outgrowth from man's own composition, and not necessarily a stranger to him at all.

When the spirit within man, the 'I', is untried and unaccustomed to its new task, its influence is hardly felt. In fact, during its early struggles to master the communities of man's personality, it becomes almost subordinate to them and often identifies itself with them to the extent of losing its own self-awareness. Man will feel that his 'I' *is* his ambition, his greed or his passion.

We will refer to the consciousness of the Creator, as the Great 'I' (it was referred to in ancient mystical script as the 'I AM'), and the individualised fraction of it, the human spirit, as the lesser 'I'. Around this individualised fraction of spirit gathers an individualised fraction of the solid chemical world, his body; and an individualised fraction of the world of ether—his electrical body; and an individualised fraction of the world of desire or attraction—his emotions; and an individualised fraction of the world of mind—his mind. All these individualised fractions collect and hold experiences, impressions and memories. This reservoir of individuality builds up and soon possesses a living entity which we know as the soul of man. The soul of man differs from the soul life in other creatures in that it possesses greater and more diverse creative potentiality and a more individualised self-consciousness.

The soul is the medium which the human spirit, the reflected purpose of God, is using. The soul is the link between spirit and body, between purpose and form. Each is impotent without the other. The soul must serve the spirit intelligently and learn itself to control the body. The personality (body, mind and emotions) must serve the soul intelligently and learn to control its component parts. In this way only can man (and his civilisation) become perfect and complete. Our conception of perfection must necessarily vary according to our own vision.

The necessity is now becoming clear for us firstly to realise what our souls actually are, and what their function is, and secondly, to what degree spirit, soul and body are as yet able to collaborate within us. It is useful also to understand the usual stages of progress in the evolution of a human being. As a rule the 'animal nature' is first mastered, and then the human nature. This means a successive mastery of the qualities of parenthood, home-protector, food-finder, and then of those of a unit in the community, a producer of both utility and art.

The practical side of the brain is next developed, and later the riot of the emotions is partly controlled. Lastly comes the unfoldment of the abstract or higher mind, which leads on from the consideration of the material and practical to the speculative and ideal, and is the door through which the soul can begin to make conscious impression.

We have already observed that the abstract mind uses the pituitary body as its centre or channel. The soul-centre is said to be in the pineal gland. This is near to the vicinity through which soul can be informed by spirit. The spirit or individuality con-

tacts the human being through the head centre, but the heart
centre is its link with the rest of the living world. Without the
warmth, radiation and collaboration of that mysterious organ,
the heart, the human entity does not 'go'—does not function,
but remains static in the *real* sense.

When the time comes that a man's body and brain have developed to the stage where the soul *could* take over control, there is
an urgent striving for this fusion. The soul begins to make itself
felt. If the man, clinging to his shell of habit and materialism,
resists this inner urge and will not recognise and respond to it,
there begins the slow struggle which builds up into the crisis we
have been discussing. The potential sovereignty of the soul is
calling against the established sovereignty of material self-
interest. The man becomes divided against himself. He fights
long and desperately.

For what will it mean? The soul desires the co-operation of
the heart. The spirit, the individuality, is inspiring the soul to the
taking over of responsibility—to becoming a law unto itself, and
no longer to be led and governed by environing circumstances
and influences. The soul desires to link with spirit through obey-
ing spiritual laws, and to do so it must escape from the thraldom
of the senses and become their master.

The desire of the soul is great, for it is near to the divine urge
of the spirit. If the personality of man defy this desire it will be
disintegrated and broken by it.

There comes a time in the life of a human being when there is
a deep revulsion against the unrealities, the compromise and the
subservience which rule his existence. The soul has grown to
adulthood and wishes to wield control and become the master of
its fate. With its growing powers it begins to struggle to influence
its coat of flesh, and its less visible coats of mind and emotion.
Hitherto these have largely been developed by the family, by
education, by environment, and by that particular development
of glandular entities striving for predominance to which we have
referred as the 'lower man'. In a former book* we studied how
any group of cells working in a specified way, such as an organ of
the body, or any emphasised or oft-repeated thought, and any
personally-made engine or work of art, soon acquires a rudimentary soul or entity of its own—so eager is all-pervading spirit for

* See *The Initiation of the World,* Rider & Co.

individualisation. Men are often aware of this phenomenon, declaring that their machines, their cars, their musical instruments have each their own personality which prefers the touch of its owner, and their own special idiosyncracies. In the same way those individual intelligences which control and guide the various marvellous functions of our glands and organs (about which we know next to nothing, and to perform which we would be quite incapable ourselves) are eager for power and experience, and are as liable to greed and self-interest, or to laziness and apathy, as are human individualities. They fight it out amongst themselves, and a certain balance of power and of glandular characteristics is established, which gives the human being his particular 'personality'.

Maybe the sex-gland entity is allowed to win this fight for supremacy, in which case he will try like a little Caesar to rule the whole of his universe, the human body. He may succeed, alas, and then the greater part of man's consciousness will dwell under this thraldom, the concern with and the cravings of sex ruling his entire life. Or the organ of the calculating lower concrete mind may gain predominance, and then the man will be obsessed, not by sex, but by the acquiring of wealth, firstly for a normal enough reason, but in time for no reason at all.

Yes, man is really a little community of entities all struggling for mastery. These entities reach adulthood and full power at various times, in accordance with the development of those particular glands or other activities which they control. The soul grows to its full strength more slowly, although this of course differs widely in individual cases. At first the soul is uninterested in the personality of the man; but later it begins to respond to and feed his growing aspiration. So eventually it leads a dual existence, serving both spirit and body in various degrees. At this stage the human being is a complex, inhibited, inspired, Jekyll-and-Hyde type—as are the majority alive today—and therefore we have a complex, inhibited, inspired, Jekyll-and-Hyde world, patterned by good and evil in chaotic confusion.

Finally comes the inevitable period wherein the fully fledged personality submits more and more to the beauty of the human soul which is wooing it in increasing measure. It begins to recoil from its absorption in personality reactions. Therefore the man's community of entities feel that they are in danger of losing their power, perhaps their existence, and in desperation they put up a fight for it. Man becomes a battlefield, torn between the thraldoms of the five senses and self-interest, and the wonderful new allegiance and adventure into the world of soul and of love. The battle may well be terrible. Man's evil geniuses rise up to confront him in a last bid for control. His hidden secrets are rooted out, his inhibitions and the hiding-places of his passions and fears are broken asunder. In bewilderment he strives in the midst of the debris, complexities and clutter of his neglected mental storehouse. He bewails the loss and destruction of so much that he holds dear. He is astounded at the chaos and the evil propensities which exist beneath his exterior of apathy and habit.

When this condition obtains in a large portion of humanity it is of course duplicated in the world also—which becomes one big battlefield, a confused strife between 'good' and 'evil' such as we see in process today.

The great crisis and battle for the mastery of the human being by his individual 'I' comes to all men eventually. Subconsciously they dread it, and at first league themselves with all their lower entities against it. The 'old ways are good enough for them'. But if they steadily resist the growing power of the spirit within them they are bound to crash—because the higher can always shatter the lower, if the latter becomes obsolete or refuses progression.

The struggle of the personality to throw off the old allegiances to the flesh and embrace the new service to spirit brings about that 'divine discontent', that time of crisis in a man's life which can either lead to the disintegration and collapse of his personality and his career, or to their enhancement into a broader, more enlightened, and inspired way of life. Destruction enters into this crisis because so many of the old ways, the old ideas, and the old habits *must* go. Until the victim has ascertained what he is to put in their place he feels denuded, outraged, lost and bewildered. The world seems a hopeless place, himself a failure, and God non-existent. Pain, distress and suffering therefore enter in.

When this crisis arrives all the legions of self-interest and of evil within the personality rise up to battle for their existence. (When we say evil we simply mean that which is deficient or in excess of the normal.) They show their ugly faces in full strength. The human being is dismayed and horrified when faced thus with these aspects of his 'lower man'. He fancies that his new aspirations have only made him worse than he was before. For, as we know, a thought or habit oft repeated becomes ensouled by a spark of life and develops into a temporary living intelligence. Man is thus eventually faced with the whole cohort of materialistic beings he has allowed to build up within his personality. If he —his soul—identifies himself with them he feels lost and overpowered. But if he clings firmly to his growing allegiance to spirit, the higher radiance will melt away the lower, and the unwanted entities will disintegrate or revert to their normal proportions and functions.

This human crisis has been much described by mystics. The 'lower man', barring the way of the aspiring soul, which suddenly rears up to do battle, has been named 'The Dweller on the Threshold'. The period of hopeless quailing in the darkness of despair in the face of this seemingly monstrous obstruction, has been named 'The Dark Night of the Soul'. The final triumph over it and entry into a fuller phase of existence is called an 'Initiation'.

All these stages can be rehearsed on a smaller scale in a man's life as his character gradually forms and strengthens. His character is the *form* of his soul, his growing individualised self, fired by the inner spark of spirit—the 'I'. His personality, on the other hand, is built up by the 'lower man', by his glandular characteristics, heredity, environment, superficial education, and so on, and is really the veil which masks his true character. The word 'personality' is derived from 'persona', meaning 'a mask'.

While the 'dark night of the soul' is lived through, the battle between the habits of evil and the will-to-good is on. It is fierce and long, and is the human personal Battle of Armageddon. Sometimes it is quite hidden, and none are aware of its existence, even the victim being ignorant of the cause of his sufferings. Sometimes it takes an outward form, and we hear of a violent character undergoing a spectacular regeneration.

It is a crisis which comes—must come—to all.

Because, as we have declared, the world is the creation of men's minds, we can clearly see that humanity as a *whole* is going through this crisis, since all the phases we have mentioned are being enacted before us on a grand scale. There is the universal will-to-progress (however misguided), resulting in the rearing up of the World Dweller on the Threshold, the terrible unleashed cruelty, barbarism and greed, which is horrifying humanity into despair at its own evil potentialities. There is the Dark Night of the Soul of Humanity, stupefied by the apparently impossible task of regeneration before it. There are the many battles now being fought out because issues *must* be decided at this stage. There is the destruction on all sides, uprooting of old ways, habits and homes; the final emergence of a determination for a better way of life, and the great change in outlook and in values which this is already bringing about.

Yes, this world is clearly the magnification of each one of us, and reflects accurately the thought and the development which goes to build it. So many of humanity are now reaching the stage of soul-adulthood. The personal battles are now taking place on all sides. That is why there is such widespread nervous disease, criticism of church and state, overthrow of conventional moralities, and enthusiasm for a thousand new movements and 'isms'. And these widespread crises in the lives of men are collectively played out on a grand scale in the 'Battle of Armageddon' emerging in the world today, a battle which has been steadily building up since well before 1914.

9

Rebirth

Let us suppose that the soul wins a decisive victory in the personal Armageddon. What actually will have taken place, and what results will be brought about?

The human being will have changed from a creature influenced and shaped by a hundred external factors, to one who is becoming influenced by and answerable to his own individuality alone. His soul being the medium through which spirit works, there will come flashes of real inspiration from divine realms, there will come moments of deep inner knowledge, awareness of Divinity, the sensing of a Plan and purpose behind human and natural evolution, and a growing desire to co-operate at the root of affairs instead of dancing like a puppet on the fringe.

Let us now suppose further : that the soul, besides winning the battle over its material thraldoms, has yearned and striven so earnestly to serve and unite with spirit, that it does become a fitting instrument for spirit to work with—then what happens? The wonderful fusion takes place for which the forces of evolution have been striving. Spirit becomes wedded to soul, and soul becomes wedded to body, and man becomes a perfected trinity, reflection of the mightier Trinity. He becomes a Son of God, which means a little God in the making, a server capable of spiritually creative work. He is linked with reality, with the world of causes, with the purpose of life. Suddenly he *knows*. Nothing else matters any more.

This wonderful destiny and achievement of man, which lies before every one of us, affects each person differently of course. Sometimes the brain cannot at first respond to it at all, and the new knowledge and awareness burn like an unexplained radiance in the heart. Sometimes the peak of achievement which is reached is only momentary, and is followed by periods of the old unrest and difficulty. But once this inner marriage has taken place there is no real going back. The person is permanently different and the difference gradually grows and takes hold until he himself becomes aware of certain fundamental changes in his character.

He has lost fear. He has lost in a great measure worry, envy, doubt, and temptation. He has lost his absorption with self. Self has become less interesting in measure as the great miracles of life unfold before him. He has lost all these things, but what has he gained? He has gained a feeling of responsibility, towards the Plan of his Creator, and towards his fellow men. He has gained a real and natural sense of unity with the rest of life. He has gained a new perspective, in which all his former personal preoccupations melt and disappear into a larger picture of growing interest, the moving panorama of evolution.

He begins to know the way he must go, the things he must do. His earnest desire is to spread this knowledge, to share what he has with others. He realises his existence in a closely interwoven sea of life, a world of beautiful, wonderful intelligencies working out the will of God. Those entities who work within his own aura become his friends and allies, in ready worship of his manifesting soul.

He realises that he has joined the ranks, however humbly, of the knowers, the disciples, the aspirants of the race. Never again can he feel lonely, never again can he feel bored, or frustrated, or without anchor or goal in his life. He will have many set-backs, he will make serious mistakes, he will succumb to temptations— but nothing will change his purpose; his feet can never turn back; he knows now his own destiny.

If he meets others who have reached the same stage as himself recognition of this is instantaneous. A loving fraternity and intimacy is at once established.

This second crisis in a man's life comes after his Armageddon has been won. It has been called the Second Birth. Christ has described it as being 'born again', and in saying that His yoke is easy to bear, and His burden light. In this second birth a man's soul is born into the spirit world, while his body is yet alive on earth. He has linked to the Kingdom of Heaven within himself.

History furnishes us with many isolated instances of those who enjoyed this felicity in great or small degree. They were the men and women who have left us eternal examples, lasting legacies of genius and of inspiration in all spheres of living. It is not difficult to call to mind some of these outstanding figures.

But something different is happening in the world today.

Instead of a chosen few battling through their personal Armageddon and emerging as triumphant servers of the spirit, we see now large numbers of humanity passing before our eyes through the stages we have described; alive to the futility of their lives, striving to find some ideal to follow, whether it bear the name of Fascism, Communism, Democracy, anarchism, or what you will; showing forth inexhaustible patience, endurance and determination in the following of their chosen ideal, be it for evil or for good; then faced with the terrible uprising of all the bad elements within their ranks, the Dweller on the Threshold! Then the horrible cruelties and inhumanities which still seem able to sway the human being as they make their final bid for rulership; the despair and horror when thus faced with inherent evil tendencies; the 'dark night of the soul' through which those most deeply embroiled, such as the aggressor nations and those deeply caught in corruption, must be passing; the desperate fighting to win their cause at any sacrifice; the final reaction and the beginnings of a yearning towards a more spiritual way of living for all mankind—all these phases of the emerging adulthood of the soul of humanity are before us now, enacting in the mightiest crisis of evolution which history has yet witnessed.

The 'second birth' through which so many people are passing in these days *must* create a 'second birth' of civilisation as a whole. It is for us to visualise, after our description of the results in a single individual, what those results will be in the entire race.

In order to do this we are now approaching the second phase of our experiment in analysis. We have run through a very simple system of self-analysis, which all of us may successfully employ, so long as we are able to be sincere and open-minded with ourselves about it. Our object has been to lay bare, however imperfectly, the average human mental make-up, its values and its attitudes, with the idea that an aggregate of such must in its sum total give us the collective make-up, values and attitudes of the human race as a whole, seen as one entity.

Our endeavour has been to make it clear that the mental, physical and spiritual contribution of each one of us has directly created the world as it is today, and that, thus, only by the intelligent and vital contribution of each one of us according to his individual capacity, will a different world ever come into existence.

PART II

WORLD ANALYSIS

10

Our World, What Is It?

Human beings move about like the veriest microbes on the surface of the earth's crust. They can penetrate a fractional distance into the skin of the great globe, but they remain largely ignorant of the conditions existing in its vast interior.

If asked whether this revolving planet is in reality a conscious sentient creature, they would laugh at such an absurd idea! Nevertheless, scientists have discovered that even a molecule of metal enjoys a definite consciousness, reacting to heat, cold, fatigue and stimulation. As for a more complicated unit, such as a cell within the human body, we find there quite a tendency towards individuality. Not only does it respond to a variety of influences—material, mental, cosmic and so on—but it evinces a distinct character of its own. We can discover greedy cells, lazy ones, industrious ones and impulsive ones, and such a tiny cell may set up influences whose limits we cannot determine.

Our earth is much in the nature of a complex cell. It contains all the elements and many compounds as found in the human cell. It has a cortex or crust, a very complicated interior in a state of combustion or chemical reaction, and is held together by an electric charge, as is the cell of the human being and the human being itself, this charge veiling the expression of the *I* or will-to-exist.

It is therefore actually illogical to presume that the earth is not a conscious entity, expressing some sort of character of its own which is as powerful in ratio to its size as is that of the tiny human cell. The cell itself would have the greatest difficulty in imagining that the vast queer-shaped body of which it is a part could be conscious and aware in the way it knows itself, but it could more easily comprehend that the greater cell-shaped body, the earth, could be so conscious! We must be careful of denying the possibility of consciousness to any entity, either because of its shape or its size.

We are bound, therefore, to consider the earth as a conscious entity, because it would be completely illogical of us to make an exception of her, or her fellow-spheres, in this respect.

Let us imagine, if we can, what form the consciousness of the earth could possibly take, and what might constitute her mediums of impression and expression.

In a human being mind permeates the body and can dwell intimately within divers of its limbs or organs. The human mind shares the body with the lesser consciousnesses inhabiting its various spheres or parts. The blood and the nervous system carry the impressions made by the mind. Or there is an alternative : the human mind may impress its own consciousness upon all the cells of its being—or it may simply represent the *collective* consciousness and mind of all those cells, or of a portion of them.

In the same way the world-body may have a mind composed of the collective consciousness of all the little mental units (human beings) within its sphere, who can be considered as the world's mind cells. Or there may be a greater world-consciousness, which we have not even taken into account, influencing us all the time.

Or these alternatives may be taking place at the same time!

Further analogies along these lines are not far to seek. In the human being the mental cells congregate and concentrate around those centres in his body which have peculiar properties and activities and run his glands and organs.

In the world-body the mental units, or people, concentrate and congregate around certain centres or places through which strong influences flow, and thereon build cities whose peculiar properties and activities rule a definite portion of the world-body, and colour and influence a certain section of the people. In this way races, nations and countries come into being, which in the world-body can be said to constitute the centres, glands and organs, whilst the continents themselves play the part of limbs.

Just as there are subtle and intrinsic differences between the cells which inhabit and produce the various organs of the body, so are there the same subtle and intrinsic differences between the races and the nations which produce differing types of culture.

Just as the varied influences and conditions inherent in different parts of the human body produce both physical and mental cells of varying calibre, refinement and potentiality, so the climatic and geological conditions in the world-body produce human units of differing calibre, refinement and potentiality.

The world-body is provided with a circulatory system very similar to that of man himself. The metabolism, consciousness, inter-communication and functioning of his being are activated in the mediums of blood, water and electricity. The circulatory system of our earth is represented by aircraft, steamship, railway and wireless, acting also in the mediums of water, of electricity, and of all those same elements and compounds which go to make up the human bloodstream. For, whereas down the bloodstream we find passing tiny vehicles of iron, carrying oxygen and giving passage to the little mind cells, analogous action is going on over the vast crust of the earth, whereon little railway engines of iron, are able, also through a process of combustion, to carry necessities and to transport little humans, or the mental cells of the earth, about their business.

Such analogies may seem quaint but they will give us an astonishingly useful focus on world evolutionary processes, and also on the degree and type of influence which men may exert, not only on their own affairs but upon major conditions on the earth.

We are becoming aware that destructive thoughts poison and destroy the tissues of the body by setting up rates of vibration foreign to well-being. We know that worry and resentment can cause rheumatism, cancer, appendicitis and other ills. Disease is due very largely to the way we think. The most malignant hereditary diseases have been known to be cured by a sufficiently strong concentration of thought or belief.

Christ said to the sick 'According to your faith be it done unto you' and 'Go, and sin no more', when He demonstrated healing, thus emphasising the mental nature of disease.

There are signs that the time is coming when this truth will be partially admitted by doctor and patient alike.

In a psychological study, such as this book, we cannot prevaricate with such a fundamental law, but must use it as the basis for much logical speculation. If the reader has endorsed our frankness so far, we feel sure that he will be with us in this.

We agree, therefore, that the mind builds the body through the quality of its control of the glandular centres and that destructive, inharmonious, exclusive, or wasteful thoughts, produce poisons, or irregular cell formation, or inhibit the cells from their natural functions of expelling toxic wastes. From this primary cause a variety of diseases, eruptions, noxious fumes, malnutrition, and lack of fertility of the tissues are set up.

Now have we any reason to suppose that the influences of such wrong mental control must necessarily be confined to the periphery of the human individual? On the contrary, we know through the development of modern sciences such as wireless that thought can traverse the earth and can wield influence upon many, as in mass hypnotism or crowd enthusiasm.

Collective thought on a large scale, such as nationalism, must indeed carry a potent electrical force. If we consider the earth herself to be a sentient living creature, then such vital thought forces are bound to affect her body and her development, to the degree that tissues in the human being are affected. In this connection we must of course take into account the whole interior of the earth, and not only her skin.

If the powerful masses of thought built up by human beings do affect the consciousness and the metabolism of the earth then what are the effects which we might expect to find?

If we closely follow our analogy with the human mind we should say that poisons were generated within the seething inner processes of the earth, that harmonious development was upset, and that disease, malnutrition, the inhibition of natural dealings with toxic wastes, and the irregular functioning of the elements would be produced.

We should then expect to see eruptions, such as earthquakes and volcanoes, droughts, storms, desert formations, and perhaps pestilence and other more subtle poisonous conditions.

It will be argued that storms and earthquakes are due to stellar influences, such as sun-spots, which impinge upon this earth. We can reply that all man's diseases are due in a certain sense to exterior conditions, but that, in fact, each man has his own unique and individual reaction to them, due to his particular mental make-up. 'One man's meat is another man's poison'!

By the same token our earth has a planetary individuality which reacts differently to the exterior influences of all other planets, because of her interior mental make-up as expressed by the collective human mind.

We have seen that in man a long battle is waged between the powers and principalities which run his system; that any individualised organ or part of his anatomy is built, developed and governed as a little community by its own directing intelligence, which intelligence is in fact a little directing entity, called an 'elemental' by students of those matters. This entity or 'elemental' is a prey to the same failings as man, and often exercises despotism, power-lust and greed, if not controlled. The health and potentiality of the human being are dependent upon an even distribution of power amongst his elementals, upon their close and generous co-operation, and upon the elimination of all predatory instincts.

Now this is a very important point having regard to our especial analysis of this planet. The planetary body is also divided into many individualised parts or organs, which we call countries, each of which is built, developed and governed as a community by its own directing intelligence, which intelligence we may conclude, in fact, to be a living, directing entity. In this case it is not called an elemental, but the 'national spirit or soul', and it would presumably be made up much as is our own psyche by ego, soul and spirit—for there is no logical reason to think that this should not be so.

It is the national spirit which keeps a nation for ever in being, and holds it to its destiny no matter how many attempts there are to overrun or exterminate it. If there were a true appreciation of national psychology and of the existence of the national soul, despotic countries would waste no time seeking to absorb or destroy a mature nation, because they would know it to be a sheer impossibility.

The national entity or spirit is a prey to the same failings as is mankind, those of fear, power-lust, greed and cruelty. This is because he draws sustenance and influence from the collective mind and desires of the nation, just as the elemental within man's body is built and coloured by the collective mentality of the cells of his domain.

Man's make-up is largely conditioned by the quality and state of interaction, and the balance of power between his elementals, due of course to the nature of his own control of them.

In the same way the world-mind will be largely conditioned by the quality, state of interaction, and balance of power between the national souls and their domains.

Life is built on a completely interlocking system of give and take, of interaction. The ruler is dependent upon and is conditioned by the ruled, and he can give to them only according to what he receives from them. The most successful ruler is he who is the best servant of the ruled. The one who wields the truest power is he who has the most to give.

These laws, although expounded to us by the great religions throughout time, have not yet been understood. The understanding of them will bring about a New Age. A dawning realisation is already coming to birth in humanity at this time. It found its first expression in the New World and in the voice of the leader of the people, Roosevelt. For that great man did of course represent the sum total of the innermost desires of his people, even though other elements had been more in evidence upon the surface. He *must* logically have represented it or he would not have existed !

If a man were to dam up the stream of his own life-blood in various parts, if he were to starve and rob the cells of his arms in order to over-nourish the cells of his legs, if he were to cover up one eye so that the other should have all the joy of seeing, we would call him a fool and say that he was deliberately injuring his health. Yet that is, in less obvious manner, the kind of thing that most people do by the way they live and think.

That is therefore also the way in which collective mankind, our world, has behaved. By systems of tariffs, taxes, customs, wars and persecutions, monopolies and restrictions, founded on the greed of the national egos, the free circulatory system of the earth has been impaired. Conditions of local malnutrition, overcrowding, thwarted expression, and over-production have produced almost continual warfare, which is the result of the fever of world disease, and of a succession of disarrangements of the true balance of power within the world body.

The conditions in the world have always been the reflection and enlargement of man's government of his own little universe, his body. The terrible distortion and confusion in world affairs which has culminated in world wars is also the exact enlargement of the state of affairs to which the aggregate of humanity have brought their development, both mental and physical, at the present time.

We are experiencing the crisis of a great world illness, the sum total of the ravages of disease amongst mankind, that crisis which comes when the result must be kill or cure.

The cure is so simple. Simple, but tremendous, utterly straightforward but difficult in measure of its simplicity.

It necessitates a clean reversal, a right-about-face in all our common aims and values—the return of the Prodigal Son.

How difficult thus to reverse our views and actions, both personal and national, to be ruled by the unqualified will to give instead of to get, to share instead of to hoard, to unite instead of to divide, to think always in terms of the whole instead of the part!

Put thus shortly its very simplicity deceives us until it seems to mean nothing at all.

But as we analyse and develop this new attitude to living which must and will come—is already, in fact, appearing—we shall uncover the potentialities and possibilities of the coming new world order. If we are able to set free our minds sufficiently to grasp and accept them, we will be faced in very truth with the prospect of an utterly new Heaven upon earth within the span of a score or so of years.

World Morality

If we can accept the idea that our planet has an individual conscious life and that humanity plays the part of her thinking mind, we can then at last conceive of mankind as being bound together in one indivisible whole, in a union which is even more subtle and profound than the outward Brotherhood of Man towards which we have been moving for so long.

The necessity for harmonious agreement and complete mental unity between all peoples becomes more obvious. Racial hatreds, hostilities and discords must do no less than produce a condition of insanity within the mind of our Mother Earth—for a mind which is divided against itself, and sets the limbs of its body to destroy one another, is of course a mad mind.

Therefore the responsibility and culpability of humanity would appear to be grave indeed if, besides living their own lives in confusion and self-destruction, they are impairing the growth and development of a great intelligence, the majesty of whose life and purpose they have not even troubled to consider. They have accepted without question the fruits of the earth and the beneficial seasons. They have seized upon all with little thanks, and treated the surface of the earth in accordance with their own selfish wants and little else.

As nations they have been at the stage where the national ego and personality rule, and not the national soul or spirit.

The planet herself, if compared with a human being, has been at the stage when she was still under the influence of the elementals ruling her organs (or countries), and a prey to their fights for power—the elementals in this case being of course the national egos. The great world-wide upheaval of 30 years ago represented the gigantic struggle for mastery between the world soul, then reaching maturity, and its 'lower nature', the national egos, who had played their part but would not willingly give up their power. By the 'national ego' we mean that part of the psyche of the nation which is akin to man's egotism—that ambition which, still attached to the material, demands sovereign rights, freedom to rob, persecute and kill, and exploit for national material gains. As in man, this ego must be transmuted and uplifted to higher standards and values, to the spiritual instead of the material, to the international instead of the national.

The world soul has developed to the point where it has linked with spirit and wishes to rule its domain according to spiritual law. The world soul has reached the point of giving battle for this ideal, because its component parts, the souls of men, have also reached that point in sufficient measure to throw down the balance and determine the action. This is because everywhere men in large numbers have been yearning towards a higher ideal, striving towards better ways than material self-seeking, to the extent that they have built the collective Forces of Light which are now arrayed against the Forces of the lower nature of men.

It was the collective aspiration of mankind which made it possible for them to be planning everywhere for a new and a better world in the very midst of their titanic struggle, not only with mechanical warfare but with the menacing 'Dweller on the Threshold' whose ogres of cruelty, cunning and rapaciousness had reared up in their very midst. What a wonderful example of courage so to build and plan in the midst of widespread disaster! Only the soul can do that—and a soul in great force—the collective soul which palpitates throughout the ranks of men.

If it is true that the world mind exists within and partakes of the consciousness of its many parts, the human mentalities, then it must be equally true that human minds can and do share in the greater consciousness of the world mind. If they understand how to orient their minds into this greater awareness, then they will see life from a much grander focus and receive inspirations of a much broader scope. This indeed appears to have been the accomplishment of all the greatest geniuses and prophets in history. They mostly thought and created in cosmic terms, so to speak, stepping-down inspirations which were almost astrological and astronomical in their origin. The work of such men as

Pythagoras, Wagner, da Vinci, and other mighty pioneers such as the Bible prophets, were surely conceived in minds of universal rather than of human type.

A coherent world will come into being only when humanity can as a whole acquire a universal way of thought. This is indeed beginning to come about, but there is a vast amount of outworn thought and habit to be broken up and disseminated before the new way of life can have free play.

It has been said that nothing upon earth is really solid except thoughts! By this it is meant that science has proved that all substances are really energy in a state of motion, and that all solids can be broken up, melted and completely altered in character by the action of heat and of other chemicals. The hardest rock or metal can be made to disappear!

Not so with thoughts. It is far more difficult and uncertain to try to dissolve, dispel or change a fixed thought, idea or habit than anything else in this so-called solid earth. Thoughts are indeed *things,* objects which defy heat, cold, chemicals and brute force, solid dangerous things which hold men in chains and inhibit the evolution of the world.

It is with them we must do battle and with them alone!

The world morality has been built up on thoughts of fighting for the self, and the self's possessions, from the individual to the nation. It has been founded on two thoughts, those of fear and distrust—fear of each other, fear of God, fear of the earth and her bounty; distrust of providence, of each other and of themselves.

Fear and distrust are both completely unnecessary and wrong thoughts, and because men have allowed them to rule undisturbed they have become as hard solid rocks barring the way to progress. For there *is* nothing to fear, and no one to distrust in actuality. There *is* sufficient space, food, work and pleasure for everyone on this earth, and as everyone desires the same things and the same conditions there *is* no real reason why they should continually prevent their manifestation.

The simple realisation of the bounty spread before them, of the help which science is giving to increase it beyond measure, of the faithful and perpetual service which the Divine Creator allows our planet to perform for us—the actual realisation of these basic facts of existence has somehow eluded humanity until this day.

Engrossed with their fears, distrusts, and envies they have kept themselves in a completely false and unnecessary condition of want, discord and hostility, which could all have passed with the days of the Stone Age.

The world morality must be founded upon two principles, which should be 'ALL FOR ALL' and 'PERFECTION FOR ALL'.

The fruits of the earth and the amenities of civilisation should be acknowledged as every man's birthright, free of any consideration whatsoever.

Any man who betrays this trust and this benefit by committing so-called crime should come to be considered as a sick man or one whose education has been at fault. All his immediate neighbours should take the blame and responsibility for the sin of the one, and share in the treatment or cure meted out to him. This cure would be in the nature of psychological readjustment and study, and would thus be of benefit to all. The nature of sin and disease being accepted as symptomatic of wrong thinking and inharmonious personal relationships, it should be the responsibility of all in his environment to restore the unfortunate delinquent to a state of harmony, content and fulfilment.

The present system of treating a 'criminal' as one who has let down the community must be reversed to the true realisation that it is the community who have in fact let him down.

World morality must be founded on the joyful understanding that we are not miserable sinners but all Sons of God, and that our true nature is good, is energetic, and is eternally progressive.

12

World Inhibitions

If the nature of mankind is essentially fine and idealistic and indomitable there must be some terribly strong obstructions which have dammed and perverted the stream of his natural expression—which have clouded and obscured the purpose of the collective world-mind.

In our task of world-analysis we must lay bare these obstructions and determine their nature. They are the solid rocks of crystallised thought of which we spoke. They are the major giant inhibitions of the world, built up from the principal inhibitions which have ruled the aggregate of men throughout history. The sad truth is that they are mostly founded on fallacies, myths and inconsistencies.

We have named their foundations as fear and distrust.

Fear for the self produces an overdeveloped sense of self-protection and of acquisitiveness. One is not content with temporary safety, but one takes defensive or offensive measures which set up an identical reaction in those against whom the measures are taken. Distrust tempts the distrusted and suggests to them to act in the manner feared.

The fearful one is not content with sufficient unto the day and for his needs, but wishes to hoard. In his growing greed he wishes to 'make profit'. Because of this the monetary system has steadily degenerated until instead of being a simple medium of unchanging values for representing goods and labour, it has been distorted out of its original purpose and made the gross instrument of exploitation, tyranny and separativeness. Money has become the emblem, not of intelligent organisation, but of man's accumulated inhibition, the ingrained habit that sets one man's hand against his brother. Money has been given an entirely false position of power which it in fact does not possess. Man has hypnotised himself with money because he has built it up to express safety and possessions for himself. Whereas, in point of fact, safety is only ensured by true personal relationships between men, and possessions only exist in terms of labour and goods.

There can exist the labour and the goods and the men who need them all in the same place, yet they are separated from one another by the false barrier of money. Unless man has a 'job' and earns money he cannot have any of the food and necessities which overcrowd the earth. Even if willing and able to work he may be refused a job—or if he has one he may be given insufficient money to ensure the health and comfort which should be his fair share of the earth's gifts. The money system has been distorted to such a pitch that it has now become the greatest impediment to progress and to a sane reconstruction of world affairs.

When we speak of money we use it as the symbol of all that men have embodied in it—power, possessions and restrictions. Finance at the present day is the embodiment of the greatest of the world inhibitions, that of false power and therefore of false restriction.

The second great inhibition is the conception of individual sin. The whole idea of sin has been distorted, just as has finance, to suit the aims of those who would wield power and control, once again through fear.

If we try with unbiased eyes to estimate the attitude of Christ towards sin, we see that He showed love and understanding to sinners and that they were precious in His sight. His parable of the Prodigal Son and of the Good Shepherd show this to be so. The sinner is one who has had the energy for action, and energy can always be turned to good account.

Christ did not condemn; He always forgave, provided there was a true and honest faith in God or the desirability of goodness and a wish for progress. The only people He condemned were the hypocrites, those who refused to face truth and dealt in deceit, because without honesty and repentance nothing can be achieved along the line of evolution.

Separative habits of thought have caused people to look upon sin or crime purely as an individual act and an individual's responsibility. Whereas, in actuality, a crime is in part due to the delinquent's ancestors, his parents, the educational authorities, the religious authorities, the agricultural authorities, the medical authorities, the community around him and the government itself. All these influences have contributed to the production of the man and his actions, just as he by his thought processes has reacted upon them also. A man's crime is the crime of his community and of his nation, and until this is realised to the full there can be no true brotherhood of men.

Crime does not require punishment but cure. The cure must be applied at the root cause—the man's environment. As for him, his interest and co-operation must be enlisted and he must study with experts through a process of simple analysis the cause and cure of his delinquency.

This is surely only common sense, but it has not yet been tried. Instead, in blind self-protection we have shut up criminals for our own immediate safety, in shame and isolation, to battle helplessly with their sad insoluble problems. To do this with a man who has 'stolen' a loaf of bread to feed his starving children makes of the community the true criminals.

Sex and marriage relationships have also been fettered and distorted by an accumulation of inhibitions. Men have been brought up to think firstly that sexual desires are 'unholy' and secondly that they are bound to give way to them! The function of marriage has been perverted by a variety of restrictions and misconceptions. Ignorant and ill-mated people are often forced to live together in poisonous frustration, whilst many of those who would make fine parents for the race are kept in unnatural celibacy because of economic restrictions which should not exist at all. The results of these conditions are seen in the madhouse, the hospitals, and in the existence of a C3 condition amongst the masses of the people, whose lives are passed in an atmosphere of alternative apathy and of unnatural stimulations, from which true *joie de vivre* is entirely missing.

The financial system bears a whole array of inhibitions in its train. The idea that all the fruits of the earth must be 'bought', and may not be given, has no real justification, particularly when the means of buying are withheld.

Because those who gain the upper hand will allow nothing to be done or given without 'profit' to themselves, and all the lesser men have copied them down to the smallest transaction, a vast vicious circle has been created in which all are equally imprisoned and befooled.

This great inhibition of 'profit and possession' is the direct cause of world wars, whilst the further stultification of the public intellect through inimical breeding conditions has rendered them mentally incapable of assessing the true situation or of perceiving its solution; and this applies to rich and poor alike.

These inhibitions find their anchor in the fixed thought that we could not manage without money as we know it today, and that neither human nature nor the present financial system could possibly be changed.

Perhaps the last of these great inhibitions with which we need deal is the one which upholds war as a glorious thing! This has been fostered throughout history, but there are definite signs that it will be the first of man's delusions to be dispelled under the influence of his growing aspirations. It is beginning to be felt that war is the primary admission of defeat and ineptitude of both governments and nations. Many of the more advanced nations have held back from warfare with a half-conscious feeling of shame and reluctance, exactly the opposite to that pugnacity which has always spurred them on in the past.

However, it is of no use for any nation to shirk her fair share in the results of the inhibitions and stupidities of all men. We all must pay the bill and meet the international debt.

But if each of us makes individual efforts to root out in future all the inhibitions from ourselves and from the rising generation, we will be doing incalculable service towards the building of a new world which, in the last analysis, must have its real foundations in the hearts and minds of the people everywhere.

13

World Responsibility

We have been thinking of our planet as a living sentient being whose body contains much the same range of elements as does that of the human creature.

Man cannot, however, live directly from the substances which compose the great mother body. They have to be subjected to the alchemy of the vegetable kingdom before he can assimilate them, and only through the service and sacrifice of this kingdom can he exist.

The vegetable kingdom itself depends upon the animal kingdom, within which we include birds, insects (who form half the animal matter on land) and fish, for its own existence. Man can subsist without feeding upon the animal kingdom, but he could not maintain life without their actual existence. They all perform a variety of functions without which the metabolism of plant life could not continue.* Their interaction is extensive and intricate, and they also act as brakes upon each other's growth, and regulate action and development in many fields.

If men do act as the mental units of the world-mind and if they depend on the vegetable kingdom for existence, then what part does the latter actually play in the world make-up when comparing it with that of a human being? And likewise what part does the animal kingdom play?

These are questions of great mystery and fascination. They may sound rather fantastic, but only because they are unusual. If we are going to cultivate an inclusive world outlook, so that we may be able to organise a successful world order, then we must truly understand the part which the four great kingdoms—

* See *The Initiation of the World,* Rider & Co.

human, animal, vegetable and mineral—play in the life of the world entity.

If man shares his mentality with the greater world conscious-ness, we have seen that he also shares it with his animal nature, containing within himself the record of all animal development, both physical and mental, as he does. If he is a truly perfect physi-cal specimen he shares a large amount of his awareness with the animal world, and his animal instincts approach a little to the perfection they attain in animal life.

It follows, therefore, that the consciousness of our planet, if it dwells within man, must also share his animal awareness, and could share it with him and with the animals too. The animal soul must be an integral part of the world soul, and must there-fore claim a considerable share in the great spiritual life which motivates the earth.

For us to ignore the importance and place of all animal life in the world scheme is tantamount to slighting one side of the nature of the great being of whose life we ourselves are a part. Such foolishness cuts us off from natural and coherent living, with results such as are now painfully obvious.

Besides his varied measures of self-destruction, man has kept up a fulsome campaign against animal life, exploiting, devour-ing, exterminating and torturing them as suited his fancy. He has done this even in the selfsame breath, as it were, of declaring himself a lover of animals, and holding them up as the friends of man.

Such Jekyll-and-Hyde methods have still further accentuated the condition of one divided against himself which exists within the world frame.

We have not enough knowledge to understand just what harm man has done to the world-life as a whole through his treatment of the animal kingdom, or what its subtler influences have been upon his own personal and communal life. But if we take logical account of the complete interaction between all that lives we must conclude it to have been extensive and fundamental.

It would seem that man has done better in his treatment of the vegetable kingdom. He has redeemed many poisonous tracts of land, and done much to help forward the growth and evolution of plant life. But he has also, by his greed and improvidence, created deserts. He has ravaged forests without replenishing and

replanting. He has over-cultivated the soil until he has bled it
white and the fertility has been lost. He has experimented with
harsh unnatural fertilisers until subtle self-poisoning has resulted. In many ways his health and the health of the animals
have been impaired by his mishandling of the vegetable kingdom. Furthermore he has wrecked, poisoned and laid waste the
countryside with warfare, so that the sum of his encouragement
towards plant life may be outmeasured by his destructiveness.

As regards the mineral kingdom, great liberties have been
taken in this realm during man's long hunt for knowledge and
for utility. The earth's crust has been scarred by mines, and men
have explored and experimented with every element of her being
in order to see what they could produce for their own benefit.
This may not have been displeasing from the earth's point of
view, because improvement in man's quality and conditions
would appear to give her better material for her own development. But when it comes to warfare the case is surely different.
Here the mineral kingdom is subjected to treatment which
is surely an outrage. Beneficent minerals and metals are used
for poisonous explosives, are disintegrated by fire and by bomb.
They are uprooted from their natural habitations, taken from
their proper sequence of beneficial functions and diffused in
strange, destructive and horrible conditions. Men who per-
petrate these things upon the generous and faithful bosom
of mother earth, blankly ignoring the life which palpitates
through her, conscious only of their little egotistic selves, are
surely piling up a subtle retribution in realms which are without the jurisdiction of any League or Unity of Nations. There
will be a score to settle with mother earth. Her methods are
known to us, even though their authorship is not. A plague, an
epidemic will sweep across the lands, a toll will be taken of life,
a toll will be taken of health, of intellect and of many another of
man's assets. They will have 'scientific explanations' for all this,
but the reason why one succumbs while his neighbour goes free
will not be so easily given. But ask mother earth—she knows!

These fantasies in which we are indulging would not seem
queer to the people of future civilisations. They will touch on
realities to which our minds are not yet equal—but realities, all
the same. We cannot deny that this earth *may* be a conscious
entity, and, that being so, that our actions in the four kingdoms

of her nature *must* have definite repercussions and results upon her. Her reactions to these results may affect us most intensively through the state of soil fertility, the occurrence of geological disturbances, the rays which emanate from her surface, the bacteria generated upon it, and in many other ways. Like blindworms we have been in the habit of accepting these conditions as 'our lot', without understanding.

But if we really are to plan a splendid new world order during the coming years, let us not think only of that fraction of the globe which our bodies compose—let us be big enough and inclusive enough to plan for a better world order in all four kingdoms of the earth. Let us show some small understanding of the unity in which we are all bound, and of our duty towards that great earth life of which we are perhaps the most responsible part.

Let our new watchwords : 'ALL FOR ALL' and 'PERFECTION FOR ALL' include those domains of animal, plant and mineral life which serve us so well, and merit guardianship and understanding at the hands of men, the so-called Lords of the Universe.

14

World Armageddon

Many people felt that the war, which really began in 1914, was the Armageddon foretold in the Bible, and prophesied by mystics from time to time since then.

It was clear that every nation on the globe was sooner or later to be fully involved, that it was a continuous world war, and that it was a struggle so titanic that there was danger of a collapse of all we know as civilisation, and a slaughter and destruction on such a scale as to cripple mankind for generations to come.

There is also the danger that even though World War II is over we may find no lasting solution to the root causes of national dissatisfactions and that a further and still greater war may darken the future. In other words, Armageddon may last, with brief lulls, from 1914 to the end of the century.

One thing is certain : it will last until the conditions which cause it are removed. In fact it has never really ceased since 1914.

In order to ascertain and estimate these conditions we must look deep below the surface symptoms of battle. We must look wide, because a world war means a world condition, and not a local one. We can readily apply our analysis of the state of a personal individual Armageddon on a greater scale to the world entity. The world soul—for, since one talks of a national soul we can surely envisage a world soul—has been growing in measure with all its component parts, our human souls. The aspirations of men have swelled the power of a greater aspiration, until finally the world soul has sounded the challenge of its battle for supremacy and rulership over all the lower powers which have been holding sway.

The challenge has reverberated throughout the ranks of men like a mighty stimulation. Many have been stimulated, but each according to his lights—for the sun brings forth the weeds as well as the good plants. In some countries men rallied to the banners of power through force and persecution. In others they rallied to the cry of retribution and justice. In yet others they resisted the stimulation, and clung to 'neutrality'. Neither Christ, Buddha, nor any other mighty leaders have set the example of neutrality where evil was concerned.

But the world mind was still divided against itself. It was torn and rent with indecisions and mixed motives. A terrible stress and strain was set up, resembling that which we studied as the crisis caused by the growing pull of the soul in a man's life. Then, just as in the individual case when the crack comes, self-destruction either in disease, madness or suicide, fought with the imminent conversion to a new way of life—so, in the greater world crisis war flared out everywhere, bringing destruction of all kinds.

And in the very midst and heart of the struggle the new way of life was appearing! Men's minds were working at it and planning for it with a courage born only from a new soul awareness, a new and inspiring spirit which was marching abroad.

The growth of this new spirit, whose first impulse brought to birth the League of Nations after the first chapter of Armageddon, has increased so that it now permeates men's hearts all around the world. If they welcome the United Nations and give it their allegiance in sufficient strength Armageddon will be over.

As soon as mankind is given over to the rulership of soul in all the activities of living, and is utterly dedicated to live by spiritual laws alone, the great world crisis will be passed for ever, and the world will be changed, just as an individual is changed by conversion.

This will bring very different conditions of life, for it has never happened before in history. It will affect not only man and his social conditions. It will affect the other three kingdoms of nature and the elements themselves. It is the youth of the world who will lead this change.

By the time the world is healed from her scars and her bloodstream is purified, new developments will come into being brought about by the phenomenon of a world unified and living as one integrated and harmonious entity. New awareness, new mental powers, new values, and a new vision will appear within the ranks of men.

These changes will be gradual. It will take long before all mankind falls into the new step. But already stupendous plans and conceptions have been declared, and have been readily accepted by the public, and the pace seems quick even to the optimistic.

Exactly what do we mean when we talk of a 'new spirit' appearing amongst the ranks of men? Are we speaking of subtle abstractions or do we refer to an actual discarnate intelligence such as the world soul? Let us see if it is possible to put forward any hypotheses about such intriguing mysteries.

A glance at history shows us that mankind has never lacked great Teachers and Saviours, Who have pointed the way like Torches to men's highest possibilities and future goal. The earliest of These are dim in the mists of time so that They are regarded almost as myths. But we do know sufficient about the greatest of Them all.

It would appear that aspiration always brings its response. The East yearned always for wisdom, and to them finally came the Buddha. He represented the planting of the seed of wisdom in the minds of men in answer to their call.

Aspiration later demanded more, and then came the Christ. He taught men their future goal of Love. He represented the planting of the seed of love in the hearts of mankind.

Both these seeds have germinated, although growth is only small as yet. But *now* men's aspiration has risen in the West, the positive and actionary side of the world. The answer to that must be the capacity properly to use Power. For Power is the most dangerous of the three attributes of Divinity—those of Will, Wisdom and Activity.

So now humanity can look for a further coming of a divine messenger, Avator, or Teacher, Whose advent will represent the planting of the seed of power in the will of mankind, the will being, as we have said, that which is nearer still to spirit than heart or mind. The seed of power will grow ultimately into the capacity properly to rule, organise and govern the whole world and control in sanity and coherence all the activities of men.

There are very many today who pray for and prepare for the 'Coming One', Whose advent may take place in quite unexpected form, and Whose visitation is anticipated for the last quarter of this century.

Already the use of power is being practised in much greater measure than hitherto. In former days we have had a Napoleon or an Alexander whose exploits have stood for an epoch in world history. Such solitary figures are dwarfed by the recent spectacle of almost a dozen giants of power on the world stage together : Roosevelt, Stalin, Chiang Kai-shek, Churchill—and their opposite numbers Hitler and Mussolini.

Any one of these would have been of sufficient stature to represent an epoch in a former age.

Power is also to the fore in the world of science. Mighty bombs and explosives, giant structures, colossal hydraulic activities which alter the very flow of great rivers; power to travel to the moon on the ethers; power to bear tremendous burdens through the air. Even the power of the human will is beginning faintly to be suspected. The term 'mind over matter' has become a commonplace of this century.

As soon as humanity has developed enough in wisdom and in love to make the next step possible, the great lesson of the wielding of power, not in small intermittent national efforts, but as a concerted and permanent undertaking for the wise control of the world as a whole, will have to be mastered. We are nearing that phase now.

It may be said : 'What nonsense! Humanity is appallingly stupid and appallingly cruel even to this day !'

This appears superficially to be the case, but it is not so in reality.

With regard to wisdom, for instance, enough real wisdom has been put into words and given to the people to end all our troubles would we but apply it. Moreover, the people have accepted it as such, have acknowledged its worth and its purpose. The wisdom taught by Christ, Buddha, Confucius, Pythagoras, and many lesser masters, has been unquestioningly accepted as the highest wisdom and the model for men's living.

Yes, the people, generally, *have* accepted wisdom. They do not live up to it because of the chains of thought habits and delusions which hold them still so fast, and which we have already analysed.

With regard to love, those who study the subject can easily

prove to us that men are infinitely more humane, warm-hearted and impersonally loving than they were fifty or a hundred years ago, while if a study is made of such conditions in the Elizabethan era, for instance, comparison is hardly possible at all. In those days torture and cruelty were merely the usual pastimes, even of children.

During the last century slavery and the working of tiny children in factory and mine, under conditions of hopeless drudgery and cruelty and want, were perpetrated on the plea of necessity. Today, some seventy-five years since, an amount of things done then would not be tolerated for a moment and would raise an immediate outcry. During this century the people have rapidly developed along altruistic lines and many have deprived themselves in order to give to the unknown needy of far away lands. Herein is true love and true brotherhood making its appearance, and this surely heralds the coming of other and finer ways of living. In fact the next great step will be the abolishment of animal slavery.

It is therefore mostly evil wishful-thinking which prompts the easy phrase 'Human nature cannot change', and it has no relation to facts.

True, there is much to be changed yet. Horrible cruelties are still habitually inflicted, for instance upon animals in the pursuit of furs, and in many other ways.

True, the wars have brought to light terrible brutal and sadistic tendencies. But whereas now it takes intensive war propaganda and certain conditions to bring out such traits, we know that in Charles Dickens's time sadism was the normal and widespread characteristic of many types of so-called respectable people.

Finally, we have postulated that the stimulation of the world crisis has roused up the lowest dregs within man's nature, and challenged the last stand of the evil elementals which are about to be overthrown. Of course, when it comes out on the surface, as in the atrocities of war, evil appears to us the more horrible, being materialists—whereas, actually, evil *committed* exhausts itself and often brings self-revulsion, whilst evil *dormant* continues to grow and wields unfathomable influences.

When scum rises, it should be the cause for grim content.

The tremendous stimulation which has roused the world from

end to end must be pouring through each one of us. We respond, all differently, according to our calibre. Many reject the stimulation and prefer to hibernate through this vital exciting period. Their time is not yet.

You and I are of a different mind, or this book would never have come into being. For remember that *you* called for this book in the first place, nothing being created except in answer to a need. If an author realises this, he loves his readers and listens for their call and their message *before* he writes his book, instead of linking up with some of them afterwards.

In this world crisis our present need is to take stock of life and find out where we stand and what the next move should be in human effort. It would seem that the best move would be to try to anticipate and understand what developments the future is likely to bring, and then shape our lives to fit the *best* of that which may be coming.

15

After Armageddon—What?

The terrible 'hot' wars were followed by the long 'cold' war, which has resolved itself into an impasse between the national giants, U.S.A. and U.S.S.R. They have bared their teeth at each other year after year. This is culminating in a struggle for bomb sites in the earth's aura, or even on the moon!

For decades the energy, time, wealth, courage, and the cream of science of these two nations has been recklessly expended on the race for the new powers which science has made possible. But instead of using them gratefully to bestow upon patient peoples a higher and finer standard of living, a rat-race has been produced which is crushing people into ever closer restrictions, so that their natural zest for living is rapidly obliterated.

Thus the bulk of humanity is continuing to go downhill, instead of being allowed to profit from a vast opportunity, both spiritual and material.

Nevertheless, whilst the obsolete element in humanity is disintegrating in a maze of minor wars and conflicts, disease and malnutrition, the newer element which is to bring in a different form of civilisation is already in evidence.

The youth of today are roused by the power of the Divine Will, which is unleashed upon the world at this momentous period in history. This, as we have mentioned before, is in preparation for the inauguration of the coming new epoch, the 'Aquarian Age' and for the reappearance of Christ amongst us to lead the way.

Very many have come to birth at this period, expressly to aid in this wonderful development. They are old souls, especially prepared for this work. They have passed the stage wherein they can be conditioned and held back in the old ruts. They look upon this world with unconditioned eyes, seeing it as it is—and they are horrified and despairing at much that they see. At first, sub-consciously, they feel that the task of world regeneration is quite beyond them, and in their recoil they seek escape in drugs and rebellion of all kinds.

But later they will gain an awareness and a vision which will enlighten them into the new age values and way of life. Even already they are quick to recognise these new values for which the world is now waiting, and which will enable men to struggle out of the obsolete ruts which still hold them prisoner so tightly.

What will these new values be?

One of them will be expressed by the giving up of national sovereignty prerogatives, little by little, to make way for a succession of unions, federations, and pacts, with the object of safe-guarding peoples and establishing international relationships on a freer and more beneficial basis.

Another of the new values will be in respect of the financial system, showing as a clear realisation of the unnecessariness and dishonesty of profit and usury, and the possibility and necessity of establishing new values in goods and labour, the *actual* wealth of a nation.

Yet another of the new values will show in a desire for and belief in simplicity for the solving of all problems, as opposed to the waning belief in the necessity for complexity and obtuseness. This championship of simplicity will be the natural outcome of the development of the public *will*—for the quality of the active will is directness, wholeness and simpleness, and the realisation that anything opposed to these attributes must make for delay and frustration.

The new values of unity, honesty and simplicity will settle most subtly into the consciousness of mankind, the while he is recover-ing from the crucifixion of Armageddon. His weariness will pre-vent him in large measure from appreciating what is happening and the extraordinary nature of the newer laws and plans which are being made with his concurrence.

Actually these new values *have* been working like yeast within man for a little while already. We can trace their symptoms by various signs. The arts, which are ever the mouthpiece of men's subconscious aspirations, therefore often expressing that which is to come, have struggled with this longing for honesty and simplicity. It has been striven for in painting, in music and in literature, sometimes by the overthrow of all existing rules and habits. It has been expressed in social life by the shaking off of many conventions.

The feeling for unity has resulted in many amalgamations and new fraternities, between religions, between professions and between the sexes. Freedom and simplicity have been sought for by the mixed cycling and hiking parties, the scores of attempts at community living, the international fraternisations between students, farmers, scientists. If we look carefully we can trace the beginnings of these new values at work amongst the people themselves, even sometimes in the teeth of government propaganda.

We could note many signs of the new spirit which is breaking through the fog of men's brains at last, stimulating them first to thought and then to discrimination. There must be scores of pioneers putting forward new and revolutionary ideas in Britain alone at present, and there is a public for them all—not just a listening public, but such an active and energetic public that it becomes possible for each pioneer to find himself at the head of a movement !

The Spirit of God, we have been told, is expressed as a Trinity —Will, Wisdom and Activity.

Of these three facets, the Wisdom-spirit sowed the world with spiritual laws and teachings which were the foundations of science, law and architecture. Later the Love-wisdom brought devotion and beauty to the fore in man's life, flowering in his arts, crafts, literature and music.

Now the spiritual-will, or Power, will bring order, control and rhythm into the world social pattern, from which, in the 'whole' sense, it has always been missing. This will mean directness, simplification, and the breaking down of thousands of barriers which we are accustomed to regard as necessary and immovable.

It is obvious that when Will, Love-wisdom and Activity can work equally together, a perfect world could certainly eventuate. This is the true goal of evolution, the pull which has precipitated the present cataclysm.

Those of us who gradually will accustom ourselves to visualise this goal and to reorient our minds to the many utterly new developments which will project us towards it, will be enabled to perform valuable service by strengthening and shaping the body of public opinion and understanding. Whether we do this by actions, by words, or by thought matters little. What does matter is that we should realise that the whole issue hangs on individual and collective development of the will.

The will is expressed in the taking of responsibility, the definite expression of a goal and ideal, and in the effort of individual reasoning thought.

We are moving towards power. But the power of today and of the future is not like the power of past times—despotic, individualistic, egotistic—for it is a power belonging to unity and therefore it must always be *power shared*.

. . . . .

In the first part of this book, the analysis of the human being, we traced human development through its many stages to the ultimate pitched battle between the spiritual and the material, to the death and dissipation of all most dear to the material self, and to the regeneration or rebirth of the new spiritual man, result of the fusion between spirit, soul and mind—between will, love and wisdom.

In the second part of our work we have recapitulated this analysis on a grander scale, as applied to the world body and the world mind, as built by the qualities of each one of its cells— ourselves.

We have traced world development through much the same stages, to the final pitched battle between the spiritual and the material, which we called the world war. We have seen the destruction and dissipation of all that is held so dear and so necessary to materialistic mankind. We are seeing the regeneration and rebirth of a new spiritual humanity. We have studied how this is coming to pass, how the heat of men's aspirations and sufferings, and the steadiness of their endurance is awakening within them their final heritage, the spiritual will, and is welding it to their already developing qualities of wisdom and of love.

Humanity is thus on the way to growing into a whole Son of God, a replica of the Creator, wherein all qualities function in union together. Human beings are on the way to becoming creators in miniature, to controlling their own fate and their environment, instead of living puppet lives, as hitherto.

Their first task will be to control and create themselves, as they desire to become, as individuals, and as the entire human family. Their second task will be intelligently to work *under* control—for one learns to control in measure only as one learns to be controlled by that which is higher than oneself. Human beings must learn to be controlled by the plan and flow of evolution and must seek for this plan in a greater consciousness than their own—that great collective consciousness, the world mind, which in its turn is informed by God.

This greater consciousness can be reached by men through their own unity with each other, of which it is built up. It can be and has been lost by them through their own disunity.

Through unity in honesty of purpose man can climb out of the present morass for ever, and can rebuild his civilisation in accordance with the Divine Plan of evolution, thus producing in actuality a Golden Age and the Kingdom of Heaven here on earth.

PART III

WISDOM IN PRACTICE

16

The New World

As one links up with the men and women who are intrinsically of goodwill and who are longing for a truly better world, the sentiment is constantly heard : 'World reconstruction *must* be founded upon spiritual principles—we must learn to live according to the laws of Christ.'

Whilst it is splendid to know that so many feel that way, it also seems sad that such phrases should be uttered as if using a new slogan, two thousand years after Christ, and ten thousand or more years after the gift of spiritual law to man !

Some people, indeed, cling to the idea that it is enough to 'love God', to attend church and to perform charitable works. Such living is *not* fully according to the instructions given to us by Christ, Who counselled us to hold before ourselves the goal of the attainment of the Gifts of the Holy Ghost. These included wisdom, clairvoyance, prophesy, healing and the gift of tongues. He said also : 'All these things which I do and more shall ye do. . . .' He had in His own life, as a perfect man and as a perfect Son of God, demonstrated to us the goal of all humanity. He gave us simple, clear and definite laws and commandments by which we could govern our lives.

To what degree have we followed these clear instructions? To what degree has the Christian Church followed them? To what degree have we insisted on our Church following them?

Surely if the Church is there to give us spiritual training she must consider these gifts of the Holy Ghost which it is our duty to try to acquire, as a work clearly within her domain. Surely this would entail training us towards the attainment of wisdom in spiritual lore, of clairvoyance or non-material vision, of prophesying or the study of evolution, of healing in its several forms, of the gift of tongues or the inspired approach to all peoples. There must be several stages by which we approach towards a worthiness of these Gifts. It would seem to be the work of the Church to give us adequate advice and training in these matters.

But the Church has avoided these vital issues. The philosophers have taken up the teaching of wisdom often in terms quite divorced from spiritual foundations. The spiritualists have taken up the study of clairvoyance. The astrologers have fumbled in the field of prophecy. The Christian Scientists and others have worked at healing. All these have been looked at more or less askance, while doing the work which the Church neglected. The latter has been drained of life because so much that should be done within her precincts is being done outside with little or no relationship to herself.

If religion is to take its real place in our lives as the guard and model and inspiration of our existence, then surely the place of the Church should be as the overseer of all our activities, the guide and criterion of our statecraft, our education and our work.

Either we are to lead spiritual lives altogether, from our government downwards, or we are to go under in the increasing confusion and ever deepening hostility which comes from not so doing. The issue has now become as clear as that.

Humanity has reached the parting of the ways, at which either they must choose henceforth to run their world in true and actual accordance with spiritual principles, or they must face the prospect, now clearly demonstrated, of racial suicide in the horrible form of mutual slaughter and despoliation.

Humanity has already made the choice. Voiced by U Thant the cry is for a new world based on spiritual and humanitarian laws. If, then, the world is at last to be organised and governed according to religious standards, the spiritual leaders must be placed in a position of guidance and guardianship over the statesmen, governments, scientists, educationalists and social reformers. This is pure common sense, although we do not as yet hear it suggested.

But who are those spiritual leaders to be? Shall we find them inside or outside the Church?

The time is approaching when the Church could assume a position of tremendous responsibility in this respect, and take on a great task of service to mankind. But is she ready and has she the requisite pioneers within her ranks?

For such spiritual leaders would have to stand by the true laws and commands of Christ for the first time in history—such commands as :

THOU SHALT NOT KILL—thus forbidding war and capital punishment, and THOU SHALT NOT COMMIT USURY—this does away with profit and interest in all money transactions.

If the Christian Church cannot, will not, or dare not uphold these and other definite commands, then it simply IS NOT a Christian Church, is it?—and laymen will have to take over its rightful tasks.

It is not that the great Churchmen are prevented from voicing Christian principles—they are in the seats of the mighty in the House of Lords. But they may be so bound up themselves in conditions contrary to those laws that their lips are sealed. The things which they should have said are being said by the Peace Societies, the Quakers and others.

Obviously the churchmen cannot stand up at this moment and denounce our fighting activities—but had the religious leaders, particularly the powerful Church of Rome, steadily trained mankind in a truly Christian way of life for the last two thousand years, the world would be a totally different place today—or at any rate it would have totally different accepted standards.

In the world of tomorrow the civilisation must be led and built by clear spiritual standards from the government right through all administrations. The true standards of *all* the great religions would, if adhered to, produce ideal social conditions. It is possible, therefore, that genuine Christianity would be able adequately to work and build and organise in conjunction with the other world religions if they each regained their own purity of form. It could also work with those of no acknowledged faith at all, who yet were, as many such are, motivated by obviously spiritual standards and ideals.

There should be no difficulty, therefore, when some form of World Government or Council is set up, in its being advised and led by acknowledged spiritual leaders by spiritual standards. Until this is so we could not count on any government so set up being capable of or likely to come, in these difficult days, to wise and adequate resolutions.

We have served Mammon for so long. The result has been disastrous. We have also tried to serve both God and Mammon most determinedly, and so the human family is now torn into a hundred pieces. By our own obstinacy we have beaten ourselves into the dust, but at last we seem to have learnt our lesson. We seem ready now to face reality, to take the hand of our Creator and go forward to our true heritage.

The belated cry is going up everywhere—'Why don't we follow Christ?'

His way is very plain; His commands have been given to us so clearly.

The Ten Commandments, bequeathed to us by God so long ago were set before us afresh by Christ, and many of their implications clarified for us by Him. We were shown the manner in which we could go forward in accordance with these implications, and also what the future would hold for those who did so.

The Ten Commandments were given not to the individual only but to the community, to the nation and to humanity as a whole. Therefore the governments and laws of Christian countries should be founded upon them. Our earliest laws were indeed founded upon them, but they have been lost sight of to a deplorable degree, and we are now largely governed by an overgrowth of materialistic compromise.

Let us therefore see how far we can get in planning and designing the future civilisation of the Christian world strictly in accordance with its professed faith.

When we have accomplished this we can next estimate how such a civilisation would compare with that which the other great religions, if also truly adhered to, could create. If we find a practical working basis on which all could plan in this way, then we shall know that a unified world civilisation founded on spiritual laws is an actual and practical possibility.

17

The Spiritual Laws

In our Old Testament we are given the Ten Commandments, in the bare and simple form in which they were proclaimed to the people by Moses.

In the New Testament Christ gave them forth again, bringing them up to date, so to speak, to fit a people many centuries further matured—but they were still in simple form as given to the masses.

The whole story does not lie here, however. Christ spoke to the people very simply of those things which they could understand, the A B C of spiritual ethics, but of the profounder aspects He spoke in parables. His disciples, who were His especial students and pupils, were privileged to ask Him for explanations of these parables. Furthermore, He reserved for them a deeper teaching than that which He gave to the throng. Even then, His words were pregnant with inner and subtler meanings, with the promise of future revelation of the mysteries of truth.

Each of the disciples understood Him according to his own type and character. John was His favourite because John was himself a mystic, a poet and an intellectual, and could come closest to the Master in understanding.

Religious teaching is not, has never been, and can never be a simple matter. It can be reduced to the simplest literary terms, and in that form it is at once straightforward for the simple man and subtle for the initiated. Its simplest terms are enough to guide humanity safely along the path to progress.

Nevertheless, such simple terms are really gateways to long vistas of ever-growing wonders and ever-growing knowledge. The keys to these gateways are sincerity and energy. The knowledge they guard is dangerous when in the hands of the unready. That is why, in every religion, the inner truths and mysteries have been guarded by the priesthood and reserved for those who gained initiation into their inner circles. The mysteries have been guarded by symbolism, parable and myth, and kept within the realm of the esoteric, which word merely means 'hidden'.

Therefore, when we come across phrases in the Bible which do not make sense, either grammatically or to our intelligence, we must realise that in its original much of it was written with a double or even treble meaning which has sometimes completely befogged a translator who was not a genuine esotericist. So that, although at times the inner meanings have survived with the translation, at other times the result has been the loss of any meaning at all!

In considering our heritage of spiritual teaching from the Christian point of view we must also remember that the Old Testament is a heritage common to other religions than our own, that there were originally other books attached to it which have since been separated from it, and that very much censorship has been exercised upon it at various times for political and other reasons.

If we bear these things in mind we can approach the Bible without that rigid orthodoxy and that materialistic clinging to the outer meaning of words which entirely prevent penetration to the inner mysteries and truths. Therefore in our study of the Ten Commandments we must include several aspects of their implications. First, we will take the original form as given to a rather primitive people by Moses. Secondly, we must consider the teaching added to each by Christ, Who brought them up to date for His day. Thirdly, we must study their connection with the Ancient Wisdom teachings. Fourthly, we must assess all this with the Gifts of the Holy Ghost, the promised fruits of keeping the Commandments. Lastly, we will consider the relationship which all this has with the fundamentals of the other great world religions.

The Ancient Wisdom, as we know from our former studies,* is the name applied to that body of teaching which lies hidden beneath all the major orthodox religions, and which has been lost or preserved according to the degree of materialism of the

* *The Initiation of The World,* Rider & Co.

priesthood. The Ancient Wisdom has come down to man from the mists of time. Its laws, principles and symbols have constituted a common language the world over, amongst the intellectuals and priests of all great civilisations. Its backbone is astrology, and its theme is the Plan of Evolution of the Universe, including our earth. It is elaborated in the Egyptian Book of the Dead, the Jewish Kaballah, the Chinese, Tibetan, Indian and many other ancient religious archives. It was of course studied by the Rabbis at the time of Christ, Who was Himself advanced in their learning at an early age.

Christ makes many allusions and references to its teachings, often speaking as of something generally known and accepted. We will give one or two instances of this as we go along. Of course there were special terms used in discussing the Ancient Wisdom and these terms occur in the Old and New Testaments. Sometimes they have been mistranslated, sometimes there have been no words applicable in translation and the result has been entirely unsatisfactory.

It is necessary to realise that a true understanding of the teaching in the New Testament is not possible without taking into account the ancient teaching that was current at the time among the priesthood and among such men as the disciples, who were making a study of spiritual lore. This teaching was, of course, the heritage of the Jews, compared with whom the Romans were newcomers and erstwhile barbarians.

The Ten Commandments had been given to man long before the time of Moses. They are found preserved on tablets of a much earlier date.

For our present study, however, we will take them as Moses spoke them; consider what Christ said about them; what the Ancient Wisdom says in their connection; and how our own future should develop in regard to them, as specified by the description of the Gifts of the Holy Ghost. We can then apply our results to the grand scale of humanity, as a unit, and finally design our World Government to fit them.

We will have occasion briefly to refer to the many instances still remaining in the New Testament which seem to deal with the teachings of the Ancient Wisdom. It must be left, of course, to the reader to form his own judgement in regard to our suggestions.

The people of Israel, freshly released from serfdom, had been kept somewhat primitive and brutalised by their treatment at the hands of the Egyptians. It seemed that at that time they could receive religion only in a crude form. They could understand only a God of Battles, a jealous God, Who accepted blood sacrifice and Who ruled by fear.

The Jews of Christ's time had matured to the point where they could be given a higher conception of God, a God of Love, of Wisdom and of Justice—no longer a tribal God, but the Father of all mankind.

The first Commandment of the God of Moses reads : 'I am the Lord thy God, which have brought thee out of the land of Egypt, out of the house of bondage. Thou shalt have no other gods before me.'

Let us hear what Christ had to say about this simple command. A Pharisee lawyer asked Him : 'Master, which is the great commandment in the law?

'Jesus said unto him : Thou shalt love the Lord thy God with all thy heart, and with all thy soul, and with all thy mind. This is the first and great commandment. And the second is like unto it : Thou shalt love thy neighbour as thyself. On these two commandments hang all the law and the prophets.'

It is thus clear that our *first* endeavour must be to love the Creator of all things with the whole of our being and put that love before the desire or love for any of the material joys of life. We must love with our hearts (which gives understanding), with our souls (which gives union with the Divine) and with our minds (which gives interpretation and application of spiritual laws to our daily lives).

An individual, a community or a world holding such a love would have only one idea—to found life upon that love, to live according to the plan and wish of the Creator; to be at one with the mind of Divinity and to act harmoniously in accordance with Its design. The laws of such a community would be strictly in line with at any rate the most obvious and clear of the commandments of God. The governments of such people would be chosen because of their expressed intention to fulfil this obligation. There would be no politicians in the present sense of the word, but only statesmen who bent all their thought to ways and means of bringing the completest possible fulfilment to their fellow men, that fulfilment being held as the possibility of developing into a true Son of God.

The Christian teaching tells us to love God with all our being, and that this love must completely rule our lives and our desires. It seems a big thing to have to achieve, a rather vague ideal for which to strive, and one needing discipline and much effort when up against the many seemingly urgent demands of our daily living.

How are we going to do it?

This is where the Ancient Wisdom can help us. All its teachings go to show the majesty of our universe, the wonder of the way in which it is planned and run, the amazing beauty of design and workmanship displayed, the miracles of vastness and of minuteness, the stupendous cycles of time and space, and finally man's astonishing capacity for understanding so much about the vast stage upon which he is set.

A study, however slight, of the Ancient Wisdom (which can be traced in its original form in old religious archives, or in its modernised version as developed by such groups as the Freemasons, the Theosophists and the Rosicrucians) cannot fail to awaken awe, reverence and homage towards the Creator of the universe, sentiments which grow perpetually as the study progresses. The undercurrent of Divine purpose is then perceived in all facets of life.

Through giving the time and trouble to search out what is known about his Creator, the student develops a definite conception of the Deity and of the Plan of Creation. He begins to love God because he has been training himself to observe the beauty and wonder of His manifestations, and his heart, mind and soul respond to the unlimited wisdom and care bestowed upon them. In studying and responding to the Wisdom of the Almighty the aspiring student links up with It, and acquires wisdom himself— the first of the Gifts of the Holy Ghost.

Christ told us that the whole of the law and the prophets hangs upon these two first commands, to love God and to love thy neighbour as thyself. Thus, therefore, the foundation of any government and of the law of the land must be upon these two principles also—love of God the Spirit within all; and of mankind, His especial manifestation on this earth.

There is a subtlety about the command : 'Thou shalt love thy neighbour as thyself' which is not at first apparent. It implies that we should, in the first place, love ourselves—a very different idea to the dismal tradition fostered by certain of the Churches that we should despise ourselves as miserable sinners. If it is only through loving God that we can understand Him, it follows that we must love ourselves in order to understand ourselves—not in a possessive way but as wonderful manifestations of Himself.

Then, to love our neighbours *as* ourselves is surely *not* the same thing as loving our neighbours *as much as we love ourselves?*— it has quite a different sense which it is important to note. If I say 'I love him as a man' it means : 'I love him because he is a man.' Therefore to 'love thy neighbour *as* thyself' surely means that you love him because he *is yourself*!! Is not this clear? We have to realise that our neighbours *are ourselves,* indivisible from us, because we are all part of a whole.

This idea strikes a dire blow at our self-pride, our individuality, our egotism, our personality triumphs and our possessiveness. Yet we are told it is only second in importance to loving God. It seems a very difficult stumbling-block to almost all of us.

Let us see how the Ancient Wisdom deals with it.

The primary command of their teachings was : 'MAN, KNOW THYSELF.' In this study of the self it is taught how the human being contains within himself a fraction and a replica of everything in the universe, from the mineral, vegetable and animal kingdoms, to the solar systems of the great spaces; a record of the whole of evolution, and the mirror of destiny's plan. He is intimately linked in his processes with all manifestations of life, and with the Intelligence behind it; and his fellow beings each share intimately with him in all these contacts.

To know himself man must understand, however slightly, the marvellous organisation of the universe, which brings to him a definite admiration and love for its Creator; and he must come to realise the potentialities and the plan for his fellow men, and all that they have gone through and will go through to achieve. This brings to birth the beginnings of a different kind of *impersonally* personal love and sympathy for one's neighbour, with whom one does actually share so closely in all the intimate wonders of existence.

'Even so,' you say, 'this matter of loving one's neighbour does present insuperable difficulties. He may be quite antipathetic to me, he may be a hypocrite, a thief, a brute; he may dislike me intensely—it would be quite unnatural for me to force myself to love him.'

Yes, on the face of it this is so. And, in fact, the simple commands of Christ seem insuperably hard to fulfil without some further help. That help is given by the Ancient Wisdom. Christ Himself said : 'Be ye wise as serpents', the serpent always having stood since the days of 'Adam' for that deeper knowledge so dangerous in unready and undedicated hands. The serpent or serpents rearing upon the forehead have represented degrees attained in the school of the Mysteries, or the Ancient Wisdom, in many old civilisations. Several degrees qualified one as a Magician, and it was three of these, the Magii, who knew enough to travel to the birthplace of the greatest Master of them all, Jesus Christ.

In a former book we studied the laws of the Ancient Wisdom,* so we need repeat but briefly. Two of the principal ones, those of Reincarnation and Karma, help us considerably to love our neighbour in a natural and understanding way, whatever he may be like. If we believe that all can learn only through their faults and mistakes, how can we condemn those faults so harshly? If we believe that we all go through the same phases of development in successive lives upon this earth, we can look with interest and sympathy on one at grips with a failing or experience, which may have been, or will one day be, our own. If we believe that violent hatreds or antipathies occur only between people who are to work out their destinies together towards ultimate harmony, then such feelings become a source of interest and conjecture and the heart, instead of being barricaded, remains open to understanding and love.

If you love your neighbour because he *is yourself,* you cannot allow him to be starved of affection or companionship, overworked, underfed, imprisoned for small offences, bullied because he is without money through no fault of his own—you can no more bear these things than if they were done to you or to your beloved. If all neighbours loved in this way their cry and their protest would weigh upon the government of the land, until all laws ensured Christian justice to men.

The first great spiritual law, the law of love of God and of

* *The Finding of The Third Eye,* Rider & Co.

man, is therefore to be striven for above all else, for it will trans-
form all else into the way of ultimate perfection. For it is the
Kingdom of Heaven immanent everywhere. 'Seek ye first the
kingdom of heaven and all else shall be added unto you.'

The second Commandment as given by Moses reads : 'Thou
shalt not make unto thee any graven image, or any likeness of
any thing that is in heaven above, or that is in the earth beneath,
or that is in the water under the earth : thou shalt not bow down
thyself to them, nor serve them; for I the Lord thy God am a
jealous God, visiting the iniquity of the fathers upon the children
unto the third and fourth generation of them that hate me; and
showing mercy unto thousands of them that love me and keep
my commandments.'

This Commandment is surely a very heavy indictment against
materialism, against the tendency of mankind to concentrate
their attention on the physical and visible phenomena of life
rather than on the impulse and purpose of life itself. If we make
an image or a painting or any other likeness of the Deity or His
works, we restrict and contract our conception of that Deity and
His works. It is possible only to represent the outer physical surface of anything when making a likeness, only a fractional part
of the whole actual life of that thing. In concentrating upon that
fractional part there is a danger that all the rest will be forgotten
and unperceived by the subtler senses.

In the same way, speech is a physical representation of
thought, but it is only possible to capture a fractional part of the
thought in words—so that speech may and does in some ways
constitute a dangerous handicap to thought. Perhaps the best
definition of genius in art and literature would be to say that it
is the capacity to capture and somehow represent in physical
medium those qualities and effects which are non-physical in
actuality.

The danger of raising a graven image to the Lord was that
the tendency would be to worship with the physical eyesight only,
instead of with the whole being, and to express that worship by
physical means alone. Such a worship could bring no spiritual
vision whatever. It is symbolic of the materialism which is liable
to run through all of life, and sets up a family habit of mind
which is inherited 'unto the third and fourth generation'.

Christ attacked materialism in very strong terms. He declared that those who would follow Him must give second place to all the joys of material life, their families and their possessions and their careers. Although He was full of love and sorrow and care for the sick, the bereaved and the dying, He made it plain that all men and women were equally His brothers and sisters, and that personal possessive ties of relationship were materialistic.

Even to His own mother He said : 'Woman, what have I to do with thee?' when His personal affection was appealed to.

Christ explained that it was easier for a camel to go through the eye of a needle than for a rich man to enter the Kingdom of Heaven. He spoke against hypocrisy and outward show. He counselled His disciples to take no thought for the morrow and for their earthly needs, 'But seek ye first the Kingdom of God and His righteousness, and all these things shall be added unto you.' If our life-motive is completely to live for the highest and the best, we attract the highest and best towards us and our lives develop accordingly.

Up to the present day men have certainly been worshipping more and more the Golden Calf of money. They have committed every crime of dishonesty, oppression, exploitation and even warfare in order to obtain it. Spiritual laws have counted with many of them not at all, and as for worshipping God before all else— the idea would convey just nothing to them.

The Ancient Wisdom teaches exactly what materialistic thinking does to man in all parts of his being; how, if he is immature, it makes him the easy prey of mass hypnotism for evil ends; how, if he is intellectual and is acquiring the 'wisdom of the serpent', materialism will lead him along the 'left hand path', the way of the Black Magician, and he will lose all sense of true values.

'Thou shalt not take the name of the Lord thy God in vain. . . .'

Thus the third of the Commandments. This was originally accepted simply as forbidding swearing and the taking of oaths. There are, however, many ways of breaking this Commandment, and history is full of examples of them. To use religion in any way as a cloak or an excuse for the perpetration of an act which is not strictly in accordance with the Ten Commandments—is to break the third one. Therefore all religious persecutions and massacres throughout history have been flagrant sins against the third Commandment. So has all hypocrisy, dishonesty or greed cloaked by religion. The implications of the Commandment are

indeed particularly wide, because all of us who are professed
Christians *have* taken the name of God in vain, if we do not keep
His commands.

Christ was more severe on hypocrisy, lying and falsity in religion than He was on many of the other Commandments, to
which we have perhaps paid more attention. He taught always
how the Commandments must be understood and fulfilled in the
spirit and not only in the letter—and spirit is always far more
all-embracing than concrete, and with unlimited implications.
We will notice this especially when He speaks of the sixth and
the tenth Commandments.

The early Jews had considered the third Commandment as
simply directed against swearing, but Christ enlightened us
much further upon it, including within its scope various mis-
deeds which have flourished ever since His time. Chief among
these have been the horrible, furious and sadistic cruelties, massacres and persecutions perpetrated in the name of the Christian
religion itself. Indeed, the mind recoils before details of the
atrocities performed in the name of the Lord, these having been
at least as bad as those committed under the aegis of any other
religion.

Our minds revert at once to the dramatic Spanish Inquisition,
but there have been equally horrifying deeds done in other countries, as for instance by the Scottish Covenanters in the seven-
teenth century, and during the persecution of the Huguenots in
France. It seems bewildering that the religion of love and for-
bearance taught to us by Christ should have been dishonoured
by humanity with such a record of horrors. But the Christian
teaching represented a mighty stimulant given to the people, and
such a stimulant, like the sun, rouses up the tares and the weeds
to flourish even before the good seed. The same kind of spiritual
stimulus is at work in the world today. The evil which responds
more quickly and violently than good because its home is more
on the astral and emotional plane and its roots are not actually
so deep, has burst upon us with a gigantic and terrifying growth.

To take the name of the Lord in vain becomes the danger of
all of us directly we admit the existence of a Creator and accept
either His Commandments or the workings of spiritual laws.

The Ancient Wisdom explains the powerful hidden strength
and effects of speech so arrestingly that the student will soon

watch his words and understand *why* he should not swear, instead of only the command that he should not. He will also learn of the inevitable results of cruelty and persecution, according to the immutable laws. 'As a man soweth so shall he reap' will be made clear to him by the Laws of Karma and Rebirth. He will soon begin to hesitate before doing anything for which he will have to suffer and strive to undo or adjust in future days. He will shrink from adding to the debts he already has to discharge to life, and from delaying his progress towards a marvellous goal. He will shrink, not from the fear or blind obedience that orthodox religion so often fosters but from a clear understanding of the folly of acting against beneficial evolutionary tides and processes. His fellow men can no longer goad him to retaliation by their attacks upon him, for he sees them not as something directed against himself, but as processes of experience and growth. He comes to look upon a seeming enemy more as upon a sparring partner, without whom one could make no progress. Boxing partners 'turn the other cheek' willingly until their work is perfected, and he begins to have a glimmering of the application of this attitude to daily life.

All the commands of Christ become illuminated, and their practicality and necessity made more plain, when they are interpreted for us by that Ancient Wisdom of which we may suspect that He was Himself an adept by the age of twelve.

18

The Ten Commandments

'Remember the Sabbath day to keep it holy.'

As we know, the number seven rules many of the processes of growth and evolution on this earth. The magnetism of the moon gives us a rhythm in which seven plays a part, and which affects the female physiology. The rhythm of seven rules many living creatures; the microbes respond to it, giving definite periods in some diseases; even the atoms come under its sway as their tables of properties clearly show.

Taking a larger view, seven rules the years also. Every seventh year a human being enters upon a different phase of his existence. At seven times seven he is completely mature.

The rhythmic control of seven does not end here, but plays throughout life unto great periods and aeons. Everything in nature repeats itself in greater or smaller measure. The day which belongs to this earth and its little passage round our sun is a tiny facsimile of a greater day, which goes to make up a greater year, completing the passage which our whole solar system makes around a vaster sun than ours. This is repeated on a still grander scale, until the ultimate day of the ultimate year of the ultimate revolution of this universe is reached—and this is a day of inconceivable length to us.

It was of such great days that we are told : 'In six days the Lord made heaven and earth, the sea, and all that in them is; and rested the seventh day : wherefore the Lord blessed the sabbath day, and hallowed it.'

We are commanded to adjust our lives according to this rhythm of seven, reserving every seventh day for occupation with spiritual matters, for the training and entertaining of the soul.

We are allowed six-sevenths of our time for devoting to our material needs. This seems hardly a fair division of time if we consider that our efforts on the sabbath are for eternal ends, as opposed to our daily concern with temporary matters! Yet this was all that the Lord demanded of us—a seventh part of our time given to Him—to rest, contemplation and joy in spiritual things.

For the things of the spirit are joyful. The linking with one's spirit brings joy—and only by experiencing joy do we know that it has been achieved. 'Holy' means 'whole'. Human completeness is dependent upon such linking. A holy-day must therefore be a day of joy—the deep, quiet unruffled joy of knowing, perceiving and giving thanks.

If one of our human friends offered to us the most exquisite gifts of beauty, of interest, of food, sleep, sunshine, occupation, companionship—if one of our human friends gave us all these things, we would be overwhelmed with gratitude and appreciation, we would probably seek his company often and offer him the best response of which we were capable.

Yet because a greater Being, God, gives us liberally of all that we need, we are inclined to take it rather for granted—even to blame Him for the mess we make of it, and treat Him as One Who has no need of nor claim to our company! It seems rather heartless, rather ungrateful and very ridiculous thus to turn our backs upon the marvellous collaboration with Divinity which has been so plainly offered to us.

Our mundane work must be done, it is true. But we should also have a clear reason for doing that work; an ideal, an ambition, a worthy goal. Every seventh day it is required of us to link up with our source, to replenish ourselves with spiritual joy and communion, to regain our truest inspiration, and to commit ourselves to the Divine Will and Purpose.

If we order our lives in this way we will be completely rounded out in our development, we will be able to guard against mistakes in our daily lives, we will avoid the death-trap of monotony and automatic living, and we will start every week feeling psychically reborn.

The command to keep Sunday as a holy-day has been publicly observed, in the letter if not in the spirit, perhaps more faithfully than any other Commandment. But joy has been very largely missing from our worship and thanksgiving. For this the Church, with its doleful voices, heavy sermons, and fearful sin-complex, has been sorely to blame. Our Church today is a cheerful place compared to its former phases, but even so it is still melancholy and forbidding. Whereas, it should radiate an atmosphere which expresses the songs of the birds, the glow of sunshine, the inspiration of genius, the warmth of endeavour, the benediction of love, and the laughter of little children. The very atmosphere of the Church should surely express a delight, a thankfulness, and an appreciation of all these things which typify God's bounty. If it did so, you could not keep the people out of it. They are drawn towards their birthright of beauty and of joy as naturally as a flower turns towards the sun.

The immeasurable profit and happiness which can inform and direct the whole life, if time is given to contemplation and study of the things of the spirit, is made manifest to us by the Ancient Wisdom, which trains those of us who are fitted to understand it, in a similar way to the secret training given by Christ to His disciples. When He raised the consciousness of His disciples to a higher plane of awareness, it was spoken of as being 'taken up into a mount—or mountain'. In this state of exaltation they saw visions, or supernatural happenings, of which they were charged to tell no man. In fact, it would appear that Peter actually penetrated the third heaven or plane, and beheld more profound secrets than any of the others did.

The time which is devoted to the life of the spirit can be one of thrilling adventure. Yet people complain of the dullness of Sundays, and after a heavy meal they rush to a cinema or any other of the ordinary weekday entertainments. The more sensible of them go out of doors and enjoy nature in company with their dear ones. But any of them would be blankly embarrassed at the mention of the real purpose and joy of Sunday, which would hardly make sense to them !

'Behold, the dead !' remarked the angel as he flew over the teeming city !

The fifth Commandment has also received but very superficial consideration.

'Honour thy father and thy mother; that thy days may be long upon the land which the Lord thy God giveth thee.'

The human father is a little replica, a reflection, or a symbol of the great Father of mankind. In his small way he has created, protected, loved and cherished. The human mother is a symbol of the bounty of the whole universe, which brings forth beauty and strength under the impulse of the creator. She represents the feminine fount of wisdom and intuition, and in her little way has reflected the spirit of Love, the quality of Divinity Itself.

If we cannot honour, revere, and cherish the faint reflections of Divinity so intimately near to us in our parents, we cannot hope to graduate to the appreciation of the vaster Fatherhood and Motherhood of Creation. If we cannot honour the very roots of our heritage we will become estranged from that heritage.

Parenthood is surely the most sacred mission upon earth. The whole future of the race depends upon what the parents have to give physically, morally and mentally. Until their profound responsibility is given full honour, a better civilisation cannot come. The degeneration and apathy to be found amongst certain of the young people of today is due to the fact that their parents had no heritage of idealism, courage and ambition to bequeath to them—because those same parents had had no such education themselves, and social conditions had taken all the heart out of them.

To 'honour thy father and thy mother' surely means to establish the function of parenthood on a grand and inspiring basis, as the only rock upon which a fine civilisation can be built.

The Ancient Wisdom has much to teach about family life. The acceptance of the doctrines of Reincarnation and Karma brings reason and justice into the conditions of an otherwise seemingly unjust and capricious world. If we believe that people are born and reborn in groups having changing relationships each with another, in order to develop through mutual reactions, in order to dissolve old enmities, strengthen old friendships, pay off old debts, and carry through the lessons of development to their fruitful end—if we believe these things, then human relationships have all a constructive and a permanent value in our eyes. If we have very bad or unkind parents we bear no resentment, realising that the initial cause of this may have been through ourselves if we are the present sufferers, and that their present attitude must be impermanent, and a phase shared by all of us at some time.

We thus can find it possible to honour our parents under any conditions, not through a forcing process on our part, but by the exercise of broad vision.

Christ taught a generation who took reincarnation for granted, as their questions show, and as He, from His answers, appears to have done also.

For instance, He asked His disciples : 'Whom do men say that I, the Son of Man, am?'

They replied : 'Some say that Thou art John the Baptist; some Elias; and others, Jeremias, or one of the prophets.' (St. Matthew xvi, 13, 14.)

Christ told them : 'Elias is come already and they knew him not.' Then the disciples understood that He spake to them of John the Baptist.

In another place Christ is quoted as saying : '. . . Among them that are born of women there hath not risen a greater than John the Baptist. . . . And if ye will receive it, this is Elias, which was for to come.'

Then again there is the story of the blind man (St. John ix, 1-2) :

'And as Jesus passed by, he saw a man which was blind from his birth.

'And his disciples asked him, saying : Master, who did sin, this man or his parents, that he was born blind?'

Obviously if a man could be *born* blind because of his own sin he must have committed it in some former time ! Christ took this assumption as perfectly natural, replying : 'Neither hath this man sinned nor his parents, but that the works of God should be made manifest in him.' He then proceeded to heal him.

However, we are told that most of the teaching on reincarnation was expurgated from the Scriptures by the Roman Church. It still remains in the other great faiths, some of which are famous for the reverence which they pay to their ancestors.

Only a nation brought up from the cradle on right ideas, fostered by enlightened and honourable parents, can have any hope of achieving greatness.

Therefore, by honouring fatherhood and motherhood wherever we find it, we will be helping to raise the standard and potentiality of the race.

The sixth Commandment simply says : 'Thou shalt not kill.'

This short command surely forbids warfare? It surely forbids capital punishment?

But does it end there? It does not say 'Thou shalt not kill *man*.' It would therefore seem to forbid all acts of killing, which would include the slaughter of animals.

We have gone into this question already. We can therefore simply say to ourselves that we *wish* and will strive for a world wherein war has become impossible through a proper world organisation; wherein capital punishment is abolished because the community have learnt to take the responsibility for a man's crime, and his cure is psychological; and wherein the natural food of man—cereals, fruits and nuts—have come into their own again and ousted his flesh-eating habits.

Some Eastern peoples have long abstained from taking the lives of animals and from eating meat. In the West we have many sects or groups who are against capital punishment, and cruelty to animals, or who are vegetarians. These people will be the vanguard of a civilisation worthy of the name.

This Commandment was also taken a step further for us by Christ. He was as interested in the thought behind our actions as in the actions themselves. He tells us that we are 'in danger of the judgment' not only if we kill but even if we are angry with our brother without a cause. Apparently, to wish a person ill may be as bad as killing him. In fact, killing by ill-wishing was actually practised by the witches of the Middle Ages to such effect that they were finally all burnt at the stake themselves by a terrified populace.

The poisonous influence of thoughts and words was well emphasised by Christ. Referring to the sixth Commandment He says : '. . . Whosoever shall say, Thou fool, shall be in danger of hell fire.' Yet ever since then Christians have been not only massacring, torturing and cruelly persecuting each other for slight variations in their doctrines, but vilifying each other to the utmost extent. And so long as the representatives of the Church herself did this, what chance of improvement had the poor layman?

Christ had many uncomfortable things to say in regard to enmity.

'Love your enemies, bless them that curse you, do good to them which despitefully use you and persecute you.' And again : 'Ye have heard that it hath been said, An eye for an eye, and a tooth for a tooth : But I say unto you, That ye resist not evil : but whosoever shall smite thee on thy right cheek, turn to him the other also.' And again : 'Judge not, that ye be not judged. For with what judgment ye judge, ye shall be judged.'

These are all simple and clear instructions, but humanity has lived in such a way that it now seems impossible to obey them. Hate, vengeance, greed and self-assertion have produced a vicious circle which has had its inevitable climax in war, from generation to generation. This accumulation of wrong thought and wrong action culminated in a world war of such frightening dimensions that humanity is finally convinced of the futility of the old ways, and desirous of finding a means of breaking the vicious circle of aggression and retribution.

Faced with the always present threat and occurrence of war, and the need of repeatedly trying to arrive at a constructive peace, many people are experiencing a sickening at the prospect of a repetition of the old forms of reparations and punishments. Perhaps they have a glimmering idea that there is something quite different that might be done, some alternative attitude that could be taken.

What could this attitude be?

The Nazis caught and perverted the world-wide inspiration towards a New World Order to suit their own ends. They perverted another emerging principle also—that of collective punishment.

To hold the community responsible for the deeds of the criminal within its ranks, is, as we have said, the true practice of citizenship. By the same token, the family of nations should hold themselves directly responsible for the delinquency of one of their number.

The whole world, therefore, must share the responsibility for the crimes of any aggressor nations. They must not judge them—they must admit their own complicity—through greed, lack of interest, lack of convictions, lack of co-operation, financial corruption and moral ineptitude.

It is a big step to take, thus to shoulder blame for the crime of another. But it is in accordance with truth and with scientific spiritual law.

If someone smites you upon your right cheek, you have to say

'I must be to blame to have caused you to feel like that towards me. I admit, therefore, that you have the right to strike again without arousing further resentment—on my part.'

Obviously, in ninety-nine out of a hundred cases the opponent would react to the fairness of this and his violence would be short-circuited, whereas resistance would have led from blow to blow. It is true that humanity has fallen so deeply into error that we have set ourselves a trap from which it appears that we can escape only by fighting. We pay for these errors by wading in blood and horror until we have learnt a better way.

We can act only upon our motives, our principles and our beliefs, so we *must* rightly develop them before we can avoid producing such results as war. Therefore our first task should be, faced with numerous outbreaks of hostilities, to attack the root of the whole trouble, within ourselves, and to rebuild our principles and our convictions upon the clear commands spoken by Christ : Thou shalt not kill—and, Thou shalt love thine enemies.

Once our life-motive, our conviction and our determination are firmly established in respect of these principles, outward events will be shaped by them, and war will never come upon us again.

Even the martial people of the Middle Ages were nearer to the conception of collective responsibility than we are today, as I think you will agree if you study the following beautiful prayer :

A PRAYER FOR THEIR ENEMIES IN THE DAYS OF QUEEN ELIZABETH

Most merciful and loving Father,
We beseech Thee most humbly, even with all our hearts,
To pour out upon our enemies with bountiful hands whatsoever things
     Thou knowest may do them good.
And chiefly a sound and uncorrupt mind,
Where-through they may know Thee and love Thee in true charity
     and with their whole heart.
And love us, Thy children, for Thy sake.
Let not their first hating of us turn to their harm,
But seeing that we cannot do them good for want of ability,
Lord, we desire their amendment and our own.
Separate them not from us by punishing them,
But join and knit them to us by Thy favourable dealing with them.
And seeing we be all ordained to be citizens of the one everlasting city,
Let us begin to enter into that way here already by mutual love,
Which may bring us right forth thither.   Amen.

The Ancient Wisdom teaches us much about hatred and violence, showing how we bind ourselves to earthly life until we learn such lessons, and how we are obliged to return again and again into incarnation until we have cleansed away all hatreds and ill feelings between ourselves and any of our fellow creatures; until we have broken the vicious circle of resentment and retribution, of misunderstanding and dislike, of criticism and intolerance.

'Ah!' many people at once exclaim, 'but Christ Himself became very angry when He whipped the money-changers from the Temple.'

True, but He had a special mission, which was His alone, to perform on this earth. He gave to all who would follow Him their clear instructions, which had nothing to do with His own actions.

If all other nations had been ready to share the blame and the responsibility immediately the aggressor nations first showed signs of discontent, unhealthy thought and activities, and had sought to discover in what they had failed them and where the remedy lay, assuredly there would have been no war. But it is only now that vague hints of such an attitude are beginning to appear—rather too late !

To 'turn the other cheek' may simply mean to admit that one has deserved in some measure the anger of the smiter; that one accepts without resentment and as a logical fact one's share of blame for all disharmony in the world.

It will only be by trying to understand the true application of Christian principles such as this, that a life-motive adequate to the building of a new age can ever be developed.

19

'Thou Shalt Not . . .'

I believe I am right in saying that the Russians, soon after the new régime had started, carried out the biggest experiment in 'free love' that has ever been tried. We do not yet know how much of what we heard about this was true. We gathered that people were encouraged to mate as and when they felt inclined, and that the children were cared for by the State. Later on, we heard that the experiment had been abandoned as a failure, because of the growing percentage of imbecile children who were being born. It will be interesting if we can learn how much truth there was in these stories.

On the face of it, if the results had been as we heard, it would not be a matter for surprise. Mating between human beings, to be complete, must exist on all levels. The soul, the emotions and the mind mould the physical from within. It seems likely that a careless parenthood in which the soul, mind and heart had played practically no part, might indeed be unable to build more than the outer shell of a child.

The spiritual commands are all based upon scientific laws. The one which is calculated to ensure faithfulness to the ties of marriage surely demands our earnest consideration, concerned as it is with the roots of our physical being, our heritage and our characters : 'Thou shalt not commit adultery.'

The whole question of sexual purity comes within the realm of this Commandment. Christ gets down to bedrock as usual when He tells us that we can be guilty of mental adultery, too.

'Whosoever looketh on a woman to lust after her hath committed adultery with her already in his heart.'

He tells us also : 'As a man thinketh in his heart so *is* he.'

One's life-motive reigns in the heart, is kept alight by the fire of the heart, and directs the circumstances of one's life through the radiations which stream from the heart. For that mind which uses the brain is the limited 'conscious mind', as we call it. Whereas, that mind which informs the heart is the limitless 'super-conscious mind', which knows all, controls all, and is linked with all life. It creates our environment and the events of our lives by the power of attraction and repulsion which it exercises. It is far truer than we dream that we actually create and build our outer lives through the secret thoughts and impulses to which we have given haven in our hearts.

If we steadily recreate our life-motive to the highest key we know, throwing out all thoughts which are not in tune with it, our sub-conscious will carry on the work and create our life-development in accordance with that life-motive. If that life-motive is fixed entirely towards success in our profession such success will inevitably be ours. If our life-motive is determined upon physical purity we will no longer attract those people to us who could lead us astray, or, if we do attract them, we will get to know only the best side of their characters.

If, on the other hand, our subconscious still harbours a secret longing for sexual indulgence, it will act as a magnet to the same thing where it exists in others, and trouble is bound to ensue.

So once more we are back to the subject of the foundations of our being, from which we launched off in this book—our life-motive! We see now how fully we have been in accordance with what Christ taught. He always emphasised the importance of a person's secret motive, belief and faith. When He healed He so often said 'According to thy faith be it done unto thee.' And with what perspicacity He railed against the hypocrisy of the Scribes and Pharisees, whose motive was that their outward piety should 'be seen of men'.

'Verily, I say unto you,' He remarked with delightful irony, 'they have their reward!' For, according to their motive, their piety *was* seen of men, but was of a quality to be unobservable by the angels.

Christ seemed more inclined to be severe on the man's share in offences against the seventh Commandment, holding him more responsible for the woman's guilt than we do at this day. There is the classic story of the woman taken in adultery, when He

faced her accusers with their own consciences, so that they all
sneaked away and left her uncondemned, as an example of this.

In our present epoch the street-woman, although despised and
condemned, is also condoned for the convenience of men whose
deliberate transgression of the commandment is looked upon as
a 'necessity of nature'. It certainly becomes a necessity of nature
if the life-motive is trained to consider it to be so. But the point
is that, by reason of such slipshod compromises, these avoidings
of the issues of the Commandment, even in our minds, result in
utter mental and moral confusion. The results of such practices
and attitudes are deterioration in health, morality and mentality,
which all contribute to give us the world conditions which we so
deplore today.

Let those who feel that the seventh Commandment is too hard
to be kept consider this last point carefully.

The Ancient Wisdom goes, of course, very deeply into the
hidden activities, potentialities and influences connected with
the sex life. It brings to light their sacred and profound nature,
and gives the student a clear realisation of their veritable importance and the tremendous power and responsibility inherent in
them. He quickly relinquishes the attitude of automatic and con-
strained obedience in these matters, for one of deliberate, willing
and interested co-operation with that part of the plan of evolution herein involved.

In fact, this phrase describes the service which the Ancient
Wisdom gives in respect of all the Commandments. The number
of people who wish to obey God with understanding instead of
in fear increases daily, because humanity is reaching adulthood
and the demands of these must be satisfied.

Let us now consider the eighth Commandment : 'Thou shalt
not steal.' I think we said enough about this in Chapter Three
to show that stealing can play its insidious part throughout the
life of an average 'respectable' person. If he exploits or makes use
of his fellow men, takes profit or dividends from the ill-paid
drudgery of others, detracts from a woman's honour, a worker's
time, a neighbour's reputation, he is actually stealing—and
stealing something which cannot be given back. There are so
many thefts outside the law ! Even a man who insists very
strongly upon his 'rights' and his 'just dues' may be in danger of
transgressing. For the greatest right a man has is his right to

serve—which means to give, not to get. His real riches, his real rights and dues, lie in the extent to which he is able to give service. Once again : 'It is easier for a camel to go through the eye of a needle than for a rich man to enter the kingdom of God,' said Christ. This seems very explicit. In fact, all that He taught was against acquisitiveness, even against care or worry for personal needs.

'Cast thy bread upon the waters, and it shall be returned to thee an hundredfold.'

The necessity for giving instead of acquiring was always emphasised in respect of all earthly things. 'It is better to give than to receive.'

But it was in discussing the acquiring of *wisdom* that Christ said, in St. Luke viii, 18 : '. . . for whosoever hath, to him shall be given; and whosoever hath not, from him shall be taken even that which he seemeth to have'—a phrase which is often quoted out of its context to give it a meaning which it did not have.

The outwardly respectable and honoured citizen who would in truth not err against the eighth Commandment must search himself very carefully—and painfully—and must be prepared to live his life with great courage.

The Ancient Wisdom teaches how the grasping of things for the self cuts off the link with the soul and its rich possessions. It explains just why and how the naked and fasting sage can enjoy bliss, riches and possessions through the world of the soul and heart—a more real and tangible world than the travesty we have made of our existence today. It explains the freedom which is attained when the *need* of possessions (more than their actual existence) is gone.

'Where thy treasure is there will thy heart be also.'

If the heart longs for the riches of love, wisdom, beauty, it will dwell with them and own them. If it longs for the things of Mammon it will certainly transgress against the Commandments in some way or another. For instance, the next on our list :

'Thou shalt not bear false witness against thy neighbour.'

It is noteworthy that this sin has been one of those singled out for inclusion in the Ten Commandments. Falsehood of any kind has always been strongly condemned. False prophets, or those who bore false witness against God, were considered to be the worst of public dangers and worthy only of death. To bear false witness against a neighbour, to cause him to be dishonoured, imprisoned, put to death, because of a lie behind which the perjurer can shelter in comparative safety, is certainly the meanest of crimes. Sometimes it is done because of personal hatred or vindictiveness. Sometimes it is done quite impersonally, because of a bribe.

Christ said : 'Inasmuch as ye have done it unto the least of these my brethren, ye have done it unto me.' This must apply to all who act so as deliberately to harm another's life in such a way.

The more obvious examples of the bearing of false witness are contemptible enough. But there are subtler aspects which may elude our condemnation. The ordinary gossip, for instance, who passes on a bit of tittle-tattle, embroidering it a little on its way, adds his or her co-operation to an activity which may in the end utterly ruin a human life, or several lives. The gossip often does his work purely out of sensationalism, but more often in order to curry favour as an amusing companion. It is done for the bribe of popularity. It is a safer occupation than that of a bribed public witness, although perhaps hardly less deadly in its results.

A habitual gossip is bound to pile up for himself a heavy debt to his fellowmen by the end of a long life. Christ instructed his disciples always carefully to watch their words. And indeed it is necessary to be a very perfect Christian before one can safely chatter away without doing somebody some harm.

In a way, wrongly to suspect anyone is to bear false witness against them in one's heart. We already know how important the thought of the heart is. If we believe the worst of a person, we are bearing false witness to them against themselves also, and we are deliberately poisoning them by the influence of our minds, drawing out the worst in them, as it is rightly called.

We could hardly do them a greater ill than this. Even if we are far away from our victim, our suspicious or condemnatory thoughts wing their way straight to him, and corrode his confidence, his faith in himself, and undermine his high resolves.

'Whosoever will say, Thou fool, shall be in danger of hell fire !'

Truly, to bear false witness against a neighbour in a public trial may be the deepest crime, because it is a deliberate attempt to defeat mankind in the effort to dispense lawful justice.

But, whereas we could bear false witness of such a public kind only a few times in our lives, we can fill our waking lives with the subtler activities of this crime which we have been considering.

If we have idle, uncontrolled, unoccupied minds, in fact, it is almost impossible to avoid so doing.

This is where the Ancient Wisdom comes to our aid in respect of this ninth Commandment. It trains us to control, exercise and occupy our minds to their fullest capacity, with the worth-while goal before us of acquiring knowledge and increasing our own capabilities as both a human and a divine being.

We come fully to realise the hidden influences of speech and thought, and we naturally begin to act according to this realisation. Words are expended energy. In silence power accumulates.

Silence is the gateway to truth. Most of us are too afraid of truth to enter in at that gateway. Hence the chatter. Hence the harm! And hence the fact that people understand so little about the responsibility of speech that it is *possible* to get them to commit the sin of bearing false witness against their neighbours.

The last Commandment is against covetousness—against that possessive, greedy, exclusive spirit which has ruined men and nations throughout history, and brought the world to the terrible impasse of this day. We are not to covet anything that is our neighbour's. Yet Christian nations have coveted and seized their neighbours' territory, perpetrating every possible atrocity upon the lawful inhabitants. From the very shadow of the Vatican the Italian soldiers went forth to massacre and to gas the innocent Abyssinians upon their own land. Their only excuse, if excuse they had, was that the Abyssinians were 'barbarians needing civilising'. Yet the Abyssinians, once victorious, heaped coals of fire upon the heads of the Italians by themselves behaving as the true Christians they are, and treating their erstwhile ravishers humanely.

We need hardly enlarge upon the more obvious aspects of covetousness. The whole world has been made painfully aware of them.

Christ, however, had uncomfortable things to say in bringing home to us the full spirit of this Commandment. For to be truly lacking in covetousness, possessions must have no hold over us at all.

'And if any man will sue thee at the law, and take away thy coat, let him have thy cloke also.'

'Give to him that asketh thee, and from him that would borrow of thee turn thou not away.'

This may sound unfeasible and unworkable under the present abnormal conditions of society. Yet there *is* more than enough for all, as we have already emphasised. If everyone obeyed these two injunctions, greed would have no cause for further existence. People would soon be making an effort only to have what they really needed—the misfortune, then, would not be in having too little but too much !

The Ancient Wisdom explains the scientific law which operates when generosity or meanness are exercised. An enlightened man comes to realise his unity with all of life, his natural birthright in the sharing of all the universe. When he becomes aware that, once his spirit is freed from preoccupation with personal possessions of any kind, he owns all things, can experience all things, know all things and be identified with all things, his only wish is to attain to such a status. Compared with such a goal, the little worldly possessions, triumphs and importances which indulge his emotional, physical or egotistical feelings, fade into complete insignificance. They do not disappear, he can enjoy them still—but they no longer really *matter,* they are no longer allowed to bar his way to freedom and to fulfilment.

If he covets still, it will be for the knowledge or experience of another, and that can hardly be appropriated except through identification or unity, in which case covetousness could not exist !

As a charming song once put it—'The best things in life are free'. Beauty, joy, love, wisdom, wonder, endeavour, fulfilment—they are the riches of life. They cannot be kept from us if we but realise it. They are to be found and enjoyed in spite of apparently adverse conditions, and even because of them. They are to be found most surely and most quickly by closely following the Ten Commandments.

That is why Christ told us that His yoke is easy, and that in His service is perfect freedom. There is no freedom like the freedom from the self, from self-seeking, self-expressing, self-assertion, and worst of all : self-justification. Let us step out of this narrow prison wherein we revolve round the self like a squirrel round a wheel, and obey the first of all commandments, which includes all the others—the command to love. But let us love with the love of God, not with our own little loves—let us try to approach His Consciousness—a universal love of a universe created, which includes all and values all in the light of evolutionary progress and from the viewpoint of eternity.

20

The Holy Ghost

In referring to the miracles which He performed and the powers which He wielded, Christ said to His disciples : 'He that believeth on me, the works that I do shall he do also; and greater works than these shall he do; because I go unto my Father.' (St. John xiv, 12.)

He told them that He bequeathed to them in His place the Holy Ghost, or Spirit, the Comforter, Who would endow them with these gifts.*

We might describe the Holy Ghost, or Divine Spirit, as that power, that Being, which lies behind the soul waiting until the soul, with its prerogative for the exercise of freewill, makes the effort to link up with It, and to link It through to the physical consciousness.

The Holy (whole) Spirit fuses all the potentialities of a man, making him 'whole', so that much which lay beneath the threshold of brain-consciousness in abeyance within the subconscious is brought through into his fully conscious mind. He develops senses beyond and extra to his ordinary five senses.

He was evidently built to exercise these extra senses eventually but his concentration on the more material side of those senses deadened his perceptions. His withdrawal from materialism in order to serve and study Christ and the spiritual laws, removes the dead-weight from his subtler perceptions and powers, until in time they are able to function.

* Actually, the Gifts of the Holy Ghost (or Spirit) are those which appear when the pituitary gland centre is awakened. The pituitary is the female aspect in the brain, as we know. The Trinity is expressed as Father (Will), Son (Love-Wisdom), and Mother (Holy Ghost or Spirit, who creates in matter; the Seven Gifts also work with the physical world). See *The Fifth Dimension*.

Christ bequeathed the gifts of the Holy Ghost to His Disciples. They in turn were qualified to assist at the initiation of their own followers into the possession of these gifts. All who whole-heartedly follow Christ even to this day eventually become disciples. In time they are able to express one or more of the gifts of the Holy Spirit. St. Paul had much to say about this in his First Epistle to the Corinthians, chapter xii :

> . . . the manifestation of the Spirit is given to every man to profit withal. . . .
> For to one is given, by the Spirit, the word of wisdom; to another the word of knowledge, by the same Spirit;
> To another faith, by the same Spirit; to another the gifts of healing, by the same Spirit;
> To another the working of miracles; to another prophecy; to another discerning of spirits; to another divers kinds of tongues; to another the interpretation of tongues;
> But all these worketh that one and the selfsame Spirit, dividing to every man severally as he will.

The first gift of the Holy Spirit is therefore wisdom. In the Bible the distinction is made between wisdom, understanding and knowledge.

We can define wisdom as the perception of the essence of all things, the awareness of the fundamental cause and purpose behind all life. Whereas understanding is different; it is the quick appreciation of contrasts, opposites and analogies—which brings deductive and creative thinking in its train.

Knowledge, the second of the holy gifts, deals with material things as such. Whilst wisdom is concerned with causes, knowledge is concerned with effects, wisdom with purpose, knowledge with activity.

Faith, the third of the gifts, is a quality of enormous power. We are told that faith no bigger than a grain of mustard seed will move mountains. In other words, it can accomplish the seemingly impossible. It is, in fact, the force which we concen-trate into our life-motive, and which creates our lives from the world of the subconscious. 'According to thy faith be it done unto thee.' It means one-pointedness.

The power of healing is exercised either by the laying-on of hands, or by the mind—mental or distant healing; or through the soul—instantaneous healing. Then there was the working of miracles, by which is meant the overcoming of the ordinary laws of nature, in cases such as the changing of water into wine; or becoming impervious to wounds or poisons; or effecting changes in the elements.

The gift of prophesying was perhaps the most valued gift of all. The destinies of nations had hung upon the words of their prophets from earliest history. A prophet was the greatest in honour in the land.

The discerning of spirits, or the power of extra vision which sees those who exist in other than 'solid matter', would be called 'clairvoyance' by us today.

The gift of tongues is, I think, the one of which least is known at the present time. A preacher with this gift could be understood by many different nationalities at once, each hearing his own tongue spoken.

The gift of interpretation also was one better understood in those days than in the present epoch, because dreams, symbols and mystical expression played a far more important part in people's lives than they do now. People were more sensitive to them and aware of their implications. Whereas the Freudians of this period have stumbled helplessly around in the welter of people's 'subconscious', a Joseph of former times became a power in the land because he was able rightly to interpret dreams.

People of the dark age from which we are fast emerging have lost their understanding of and appreciation for these mystical or so-called magical gifts, and of their place in human development. It is interesting to note that they had been known and practised throughout history in both their good and bad, white and black, spiritual and demoniac forms. But it was Christ Who firmly established them and gave them their true value as the greatest heritage of the perfect spiritual life.

These gifts, therefore, must come within the responsibility and the activities of the Church herself. Surely it is in the neglect of this function that she has failed us, if failed us she has? For many generations she has practically ignored our potentialities in respect of these gifts. She has left their development to the hazards of the layman's powers.

What has the Church had to say or do in connection with our attainment of these gifts? By the Middle Ages, they had been debased, misused and directed into the channels of 'Black

Magic' by the instinctive efforts of the layman, as well as by the more sophisticated members of the Church. Whilst the Church, neglectful, grew ever more corrupt and worldly, the common people became honeycombed with witches and sorcerers, who finally scared them so much that they burnt them in their thousands at the stake.

After that prophecy was left to the subtler efforts of our poets and writers—wonderful men but without enough authority. At present prophecy is left to our mushroom-growth of astrologers and fortune-tellers, and is punishable by imprisonment!

That which should be the most sacred function enthroned at the core of the Church is now punishable by imprisonment, without any understanding or explanations given!

The gift of healing is practised in various forms by laymen who feel their birthright striving within them. But they have to struggle along without the help, instruction and protection from the Church which is their due, or from the medical profession in whose province their work also lies.

The gift of clairvoyance is exercised in varying degrees and in a variety of ways. It was used as a semi-scientific experiment in the early days of the spiritualists. However, the sincerity of many of its adherents has brought them to establish it in its true place in the Christian life. They have practically built up their own Spiritualist Christian Church, having been obliged to work outside their real home, the orthodox Christian Church.

The Ancient Wisdom gave full and explicit teachings in regard to the gifts of the Holy Ghost, or Divine Spirit in man. These teachings were concealed within the original symbolic language of the Christian Bible, within the Jewish Kaballah, the Egyptian and Tibetan Books of the Dead, the Chinese Yih-King, the Indian Vedas, the Hieroglyphics of Mexico and Peru, the symbolism of the ancient Druids—in fact they can be discovered in the archives of all ancient and powerful priesthoods. In the Middle Ages constant warfare had caused the priests of many lands to conceal their precious archives far from the ken of the layman. It was the practice of the conquerors always to burn or steal the treasured libraries and archives of the vanquished, conscious that therein lay the power of their prisoners and that their best hope of exercising tyranny lay in keeping them ignorant. (Hitler revised this barbaric theory and practice in our own times.)

The teachings of the Ancient Wisdom were successively expurgated and forbidden for reasons of worldly policy, until the existence of the secret lore faded more and more from the memory of common men. It was kept alive, however, by faithful adherents under many guises—in alchemy, freemasonry, occultism, the flame of knowledge was tended and kept burning as we know.

At last, towards the ending of the Dark Age, that is to say at the finish of the nineteenth century, it began to emerge again into the light of day. The time had come for wisdom and knowledge to be offered to the people once more. So the descendants of the secret fraternities came out into the open one by one, and a flood of occult literature was set free upon the public mind.

Madame H. P. Blavatsky wrote her amazing classics, including the famous *Secret Doctrine*; the modern Theosophists were established : the Rosicrucians and other fraternities began to give out their teachings little by little to the public. The schools of spiritualism and Christian Science arose. The people had begun to seek the knowledge, so long denied them, for themselves. They had by-passed the Church, as it were, and left her behind in their sudden race for personal progress. She was stuck so deeply in her habitual ruts that for a long while she ignored what was happening, except for an attitude of vague condemnation. But the murmur of the awakening of the people rose to an outcry, when, after much mental experimentation, they came to realise that the things which they had been discovering in byways and odd places should have been given to them by their Church.

They turned from the Church. Then they turned *on* the Church.

'The Church has failed us ! The Church is dead—her day is past !' they said.

This stimulating challenge is beginning to bear ripe fruit. For, of course, the Church represents not only religion but the *quality* of the peoples' demand for it.

The Christian Church has now a very stiff mountain to climb in order to gain the summit whereon she should truly be enthroned. This mountain is composed of the actual knowledge and understanding and upholding of her own teachings ! Let us wish her a quick mounting and help her all we can.

The Ancient Wisdom is represented today in the West in fragments—some spurious, some genuine, some naïve, noisy and amateur, others deeper, silent and unnoticed. Under the names of occultism, mysticism, theosophy, spiritualism and many other 'isms', its teachings are being tried out. In its rapid progress orthodox science, medicine and psychology, are crossing the boundaries into the sphere of the mysteries. Soon all will meet and fuse in spite of false barriers. The interesting thing is that all these studies and experiments, if performed by honest, spiritually-oriented and selfless people, are direct routes to the attainment of the gifts of the Holy Ghost.

The Ancient Wisdom offers a rich store of teaching which is understood little by little. It indicates the gateway to wisdom, and the acquiring of knowledge, providing the foundations from which the Path of Attainment may be attempted. The spiritualists and other 'mediums' are busy developing clairvoyance—'the discerning of spirits'—and studying the extra-senses and their development. Healing is being developed and practised very widely. Miracles are seriously being attempted. Prophecy and interpretation are widely misused by a crude mass-production of astrologers who, rushing in where the Church fears to tread, try to satisfy the blind urge and demand of the people for those gifts.

Much of all this is cheap, crude, meretricious.

Some of it is not.

Lacking is a true home, a firm centre, a fountain-head for all these scattered efforts. That centre should be the Church.

St. Paul said that 'all these gifts are of no avail without charity [or love]'. . . . Faith, hope and charity, but the greatest of these is charity.'

The Church should be the channel and the floodgate of Faith, Hope and Charity, binding together in their flow, in understanding and safety, the courageous and sturdy efforts of the people everywhere to reach their own heritage for themselves.

21

World Faiths

This book has been written in a Christian country, by one belonging to the Christian faith.

There is no reason, however, for it to be considered as expressing the Christian viewpoint only. There is no reason for it to be considered as applying only to the country of its origin. These pages could have been written from the viewpoint of any other country or faith in the world, with only the most superficial of alterations.

The differences between races are sometimes due to climate, and often due to developments of personality. Therefore the first part of this book would have to be written a little differently for each country, emphasising for each one their particular personality limitations and inhibitions, the differing standards and values set for the activities of everyday life. Certain subjects which produce strong inhibitions in the English temperament would hardly enter into the consciousness of another race at all —and vice versa. Diversity is always most marked on the surface of life.

On the other hand, the study of spiritual laws deals with the soul and spirit of man, which we recognise as being bound in inner unity one and all. Therefore, logically, there must be in the last analysis one fundamental set of spiritual laws for all mankind. This is a tremendously important point to realise. It means that the last part of this book applies equally to all races. It means that all true religions must be built upon the same simple foundations. Uncover these foundations and all may meet upon the same moral basis; all may build together with perfect agreement at world reconstruction.

Christ uncovered the letter to show us the spirit of the Ten

Commandments. He emphasised the single rule of Love upon which they all hang. I believe that if the same were done for the complement of the Ten Commandments in the other great world religions we should find that underneath the letter was the self-same spirit. I believe that, starting from fundamentals, it would be possible to set up a simple table of first principles which would be inherent in all the world faiths and which would represent their pure foundations. And since the Ancient Wisdom and the world faiths are all grounded in the same roots, such a table of first principles could and would include the Mystery Schools, and would thus link all seekers after truth in one fraternity and one code.

Would it be a useful thing to formulate such a set of spiritual principles common to us all? Yes, it would. Differences in religious doctrines have caused perhaps more cruelty and warfare than anything else in history. This is due to men's materialism and their tendency to stress always the outer letter of the teaching and its outward trappings. Materialism will die but slowly. Men can be safeguarded against its insidious effects only by having a constant clear reminder before them of those fundamentals to which they wish to give allegiance.

It would need another book in which to prove our contention that the spiritual laws as taught by Christ exist at the root of all other religions. We can only lay the claim here, and give perhaps one or two examples.

The establishment of such a universal spiritual code to which all could subscribe would be of inestimable value at this time of all times. President Roosevelt, Winston Churchill, Chiang Kai-shek and other leaders of yesterday were actually subscribing to such a code when they established the Atlantic Charter. Now people everywhere should give the United Nations understanding and support; in order that all progressive ideas and plans may be tested up against such a code, and the old insidious evils which always entrap us in spite of good resolves be kept firmly at bay.

The first principle, that of loving the Creator with all one's being, certainly exists in all faiths, which all bow down, and ever have done, to the One God above all other gods. This is a truth not always realised. People of all faiths can meet at once on this principle. The United Nations Charter subscribes to it by the expressed ideal of establishing the future organisation of the world upon spiritual foundations.

Christ emphasised as the second essential the love of one's neighbour. This principle also is easily uncovered in all religions. The unity of humanity, the brotherhood of man, have been declared until their meaning is submerged by repetition.

The United Nations Charter makes clear the intention that the brotherhood of mankind shall become a fact in living—that all men shall have an equal chance in life, freedom from fear and want, a choice in their own form of government; in fact, an assurance that all of God's gifts shall be shared between neighbours, individual and national.

The Atlantic Charter further made a stand for the sixth Commandment—Thou shalt not kill. In it Roosevelt and Churchill stated that they 'believe that all the nations of the world, for realistic as well as spiritual reasons, must come to the abandonment of the use of force'. This is a grand improvement, surely, on the former habit of glorifying war.

The Commandments against stealing and coveting are also looked after by the Atlantic Charter, which proposes to strive for 'improved labour standards, economic adjustment and social security'—thus preventing, if successful, the temptation to these sins.

Thus the Atlantic Charter, even in its earliest and simplest form, *endorses at least six of the Ten Commandments—and is also carefully calculated to obtain the support of all the races and religions of the world!* Here is a point of the most profound significance.

Our two fine war leaders, Christian leaders of Christian lands, began to build up the spiritual code, which we have just envisaged, in the form of the Atlantic Charter. It is true that the leaders and sovereigns who at once rallied to its support were outstandingly Christian—Queen Wilhelmina, Chiang Kai-shek, Emperor Haile Selassie—Christians of many races and colours. But the Atlantic Charter itself does not bear the label of Christianity. It is a plan, an ideal and a code for all peoples of all faiths and it can be claimed and endorsed equally by them all.

We have here the foundation not of a world religion but of a world spiritual code, standard and plan, which in the last analysis is religion in *practice,* and to which all faiths could subscribe. We have here a practical scheme for the living of one's religion on a universal scale. It is wisdom in practice too. It gives us the bare foundations upon which a new civilisation and a Golden Age could be built.

This, of course, was said before when the League of Nations came into being. But the foundations of a new age cannot be so quickly laid. They have to be endorsed, upheld and striven for by the people in their strength before they can take firm root. The League of Nations represented the first germ of a great idea, the first flash of a new vision. The people were not quite ready for it. They were not prepared to make individual effort for it. Now things have changed, with the formation of the United Nations.

But it will be necessary for the people everywhere to do two things. Firstly, to face the fundamentals of their own religion. Secondly, to seek how they may be applied to daily living, individually, collectively and internationally. They must do this with as much fervour, endurance and steadfastness as it has hitherto needed war to bring forth.

Once a permanent flame of endeavour has been set alight in men's hearts war will no longer be necessary, for they will have enough inspiration to find other and better solutions for their difficulties.

When once such a universal spiritual code, as is subconsciously adhered to in the United Nations Charter, is set up and defined before all the world, the fundamental spiritual unity of all mankind will become a realised fact, as will also be the oneness of the bases of all religions.

When this happens, the present valiant efforts to bring orthodox religions together to smooth over their differences and persuade them to be friendly to each other (that such a necessity should arise between religions!) will take its place as a superficial rather than a fundamental activity. The extreme difficulty and discouragement which noble efforts such as the World Fellowship of Faiths have endured is due to the fact that they were unfortunately not concerned with the fundamentals of all spirituality in *practice,* which is what men in their hearts were longing for.

Let us get down to these fundamentals and decide what kind of a world *all* our religions in their purest form would produce, and keep that vision well to the fore. Superficial doctrinal differences would soon fade into insignificance.

We shall soon be rewarded if we seek for fundamentals in the wealth of the literature of the principal world faiths.

In the Buddhist Scriptures, for instance, the teaching of Buddha is summed up in a passage which would blend perfectly with the Sermon on the Mount. It reads :

> Let us live happily, not hating those who hate us; let us live free from hatred among men who hate.
>
> For never does hatred cease by hatred, hatred ceases by love; this is always its nature.
>
> Let us, therefore, overcome anger by kindness, evil by good, falsehood by truth.
>
> Let us speak the truth; yield not to anger; give when asked, even from the little that we have.
>
> By these things shall we enter the presence of the gods.

Then again, in the famous Chinese Bible of the Taoists, the Tao Teh King, we find this saying of Lao Tze :

> I have three precious things which I hold fast and prize : the first is gentleness; the second is frugality; the third is humility, which keeps me from putting myself before others.
>
> Be gentle and you can be bold; be frugal, and you can be liberal; avoid putting yourself before others, and you can become a leader of men.
>
> Gentleness brings victory to him who attacks, and safety to him who defends. Those whom Heaven would save, it fences round with gentleness.
>
> The greatest conquerors are those who overcome their enemies without strife.

It is good to think that teeming millions in the East have these ideals as their true spiritual background.

Turning to India we can select a passage from the *Bhagavad Gîta* which exactly sums up all I have written in Chapter Eight about the personal Armageddon, and shows how the sages of those early days perfectly understood and studied the intricacies of spiritual psychology. It is from a translation by Sir Edwin Arnold and reads :

> Let each man raise
> The Self by Soul, not trample down his Self,
> Since Soul that is Self's friend may grow Self's foe,
> Soul is Self's friend when Self doth rule o'er Self.
> But Self turns enemy if Soul's own self
> Hates Self as not itself.

This wonderful translation of most subtle thought has cap-
tured in a few lines the secret which has eluded the psychoanalysts for a generation. You are perhaps beginning to agree
with me that this book could have been written indeed from the
viewpoint of other lands and other faiths?

Let us turn now to Confucius. When asked by a disciple : 'Can
one word cover the whole duty of man?' the sage replied :

'Fellow-feeling, perhaps. Do not do unto others what thou
wouldst not they should do unto thee.'

In all religions the fundamentals in their purity and simplicity
are the same. The overlay of orthodoxy, tradition, corruption
and distortion which has encrusted most of them, obscuring their
life-motive in the same way that a human being's life-motive is
obscured, can be broken down and cast away, just as can be the
inhibitions of the individual man.

We have shown how a person can be analysed and his true life-
motive built up and brought to the fore to rule his life. We have
shown how the same process can be exercised for a nation. Just
so must it also be applied to the religions which have almost
become embodied, as it were, in the solid thought-form of habit.

By going straight to the heart of all great religions, rooting that
heart out and exposing its beauty and simplicity and its practical
merit, we shall surely find the basis for our brotherhood of man,
for we shall find the one and selfsame spiritual code everywhere,
that code whose keyword is Love.

This code can be the meeting-place for all men in their efforts
to build a new world. This code has been resolved into practical
form, into universal application, for the first time in history by
the Atlantic Charter.

Let us try to grasp the epoch-making significance of this. Let
us fit ourselves and our children to take up this challenge and
this chance, and so turn the page for ever upon the Dark Age of
human history just drawing to a close, the 'Night of the Soul' of
all humanity.

22

Summing Up

We have now come to the end of our voyage of discovery. It is time to summarise our results as clearly as we may.

In our process of self-analysis we uncovered many things. Perhaps the most important was the average man's complete lack of any realisation of his own power, responsibility and place in the scheme of things. Someone has called man a frightened God. If, as we have been told, we really are potential Gods (sons of the One God) then we certainly are living with our heads stuck in the sand for most of our lives, because we usually neither see, suspect nor want to know about or believe in that Godhead. Our Path to Godhood has been defined by Christ. The steps to its achievement have been described by Him and by St. Paul as the gifts of the Holy Ghost. A searching and exhaustive teaching about this Path or Way to God, which exists in all religions, has been bequeathed to us by the sages of a past Golden Age in the archives of the Ancient Wisdom.

One and all declare that the rule of Love, universal Love, will lead us to a new civilisation undreamt of in its beauty, and to our own fulfilment.

To put Wisdom into practice is really to put Love into practice because Wisdom and Love are one—true Love cannot be exercised without awakening Wisdom in the heart. Such Wisdom will control our choice of knowledge, and will build the outer circumstances of our lives.

We have seen how each human being must play a necessary part in the World Body, and could have power to wield a thought which could complete or mar the perfect whole. We cannot see or know which of the seemingly unimportant people around us is wielding powerful creative influences in the hidden realms of the thought world. Even a lunatic raging in an asylum *may* have lost his physical reason because of a superhuman effort his super-conscious mind is continually making for the good of his fellow men. Even a Hitler or a Mussolini may, in a back-handed way, rouse up the world to a much-needed regeneration.

Let us reserve our judgement about all things while we try to see the picture whole. For we are very far from Wisdom yet. It is indeed something which we might not recognise when we at first glimpse it.

Our initial effort in these chapters was to try to bring home responsibility for world conditions to each one of us individually. Our second effort was to show how that individual influence worked out collectively in the whole of humanity—the World Body, and of how there may be an interchange of influences between the World Being or Intelligence, and the units or cells of Its mind, the human intellects. We envisaged that great sea of creative mind in which we move and which we mould and fashion secretly with our thoughts. We made it clear that only a change of thought here and now within each one of us, however obscure, can bring about a better world and a new civilisation; and that such thought definitely *can* bring it about and in fact is already doing so.

We have shown that there is nothing holding us back except our massive inhibitions, our lack of developed life-motive and the creative mind which it produces. All the teaching, all the laws we require are there awaiting us, have always been there. Humanity has been shepherded along throughout its history by one great teacher after another, each one taking it forward to a more advanced and subtler teaching. Thus in the school of life there have been successive masters for humanity's guidance until the Christ came. He, Master of all the Masters, as the Secret Wisdom teaches, came to bring us the great Initiation of the heart.

Some good and earnest people who have for the first time visioned the possibility of a World Spiritual Fraternity try to level all the teachers together as equals in their efforts to be 'fair all round'. They talk of Jesus, Mahomet and Pythagoras, for instance, as if they were men of the same spiritual stature. This shows deplorable ignorance. Even in a college the headmaster is never put on a level with the kindergarten master or even the padre. Their distinctive qualifications, functions and spheres of influence are fully appreciated by the youngest of students. The Masters of the World School of Life play also their definite and different parts as they guide the various races of humanity along the path of Evolution. Christ spoke often of a coming period in the world's history when again the great One would appear amongst men—the Son of Man.

There are many thousands today who are awaiting the 'Ever-coming One', the Christ, as I think they would tell us, One who is to bring yet another quality and yet another task to the endeavour of man.

Meanwhile, it is not sufficient for us to be progressively-minded. We must be *intelligently* progressive too! We must try to see the course of evolution whole, in which, as the 'child is father to the man', so the past is father to the future, and thus shows us the way. The ideals held up before humanity by one teacher after another, so seemingly impossible of fulfilment at the time, have been indeed the mirror to the future, showing us the proud goal of our existence.

The last and finest ideal was the simple rule of Love which Christ gave to us, not as an impossible delusion but as a picture of the future of mankind.

Let us see how life will work out when you and I and all of us have grown sufficiently to Love—a time that is not too far ahead now.

Love implies trust. A true love of our Creator would include an absolute trust in His bounty, His care, and His plan for us.

Whether our idea of the Creator of this universe visions Him in the form of a super-super human being, or visions Him as a formless Intelligence permeating all life, matters little, so long as we admit that some purposeful Intelligence must have designed and set in motion this universe, and has obviously some plan which is working out on too grand a scale for our limited vision to encompass. If we cannot trust the Intelligence which designed a kitten, a child, a sunset and an atom, and which has filled this earth with every conceivable gift for the enjoyment of all its creatures, then we are of little account. We can surely give at least that much response to all we have—the response of trust which is a part of love.

The moment that we do utterly trust the Father of this universe the scales fall from our eyes. We then see, not only that there is more than enough bounty in this world for us all—but that our physical needs are far fewer than we had supposed— they dwindle in importance before the riches gained through love and trust.

If we trust the Father we must trust the processes of evolution which He has designed for us—we must trust the phases, the trials and errors, the stages through which these processes take our fellow men and ourselves. We must trust and love these fellowmen because they are a careful and precious creation of that same Maker of sunsets. It will no longer be with us a question of tolerance towards any of them, but one of acceptance, understanding and love.

To understand—that is our great need.

Wars have been fought not only because the aggressor nations possessed power-lust, cruelty and tyranny, but because the other nations did *not* possess certain necessary qualities. They did not possess convictions, loyalty, unity, co-operation and courage, or wars could have been prevented at the start. They did not possess enough love, understanding and responsibility, or wars need never have threatened at all.

When the 'pacific' nations have learnt to take at least half the blame for wars they will have developed enough understanding to build a better world.

What is the answer, then, to this plea for love, trust and understanding?

The answer is *sharing*—looking upon all things in life as everyone's heritage and everyone's due.

No question of giving—these things are no one's to give—a question merely of responsibility—undertaking to see that everyone gets his share and everyone gets an equal chance.

How can this be done?

Only through central representative organisation—through a World Council or Government, on the one hand, and through full public co-operation on the other.

This suggestion, which would have appeared purely Utopian and dangerous a few years ago, has now come to be largely accepted as not only a practical solution of world difficulties but as possible of development in the near future.

In spite, therefore, of the scum of evil which is boiling so furiously at the surface of world conditions today, the ideal which Buddha held out to humanity of the Wisdom of the heart, and the ideal which Christ held out to humanity of the Love of the heart, produce for us a vision and a goal more near of realisation than ever before.

This is because we are now seeing the youth in every land inspired by the need for love, beauty and peacefulness; for freedom of expression and for ways of living which will produce a very different world to the one in which they find themselves today. It is also because the older generation, caught in an impasse of muddle, antagonisms, injustices and apathy, are also feeling so desperate that some of them are becoming ready, not only to throw in their lot with the revolting young, but to respect and accept their attitude towards existing conditions, and even to seek, hopefully, their aid and any new ideas which they may bring to the situation.

But, although so many desperately realise the necessity for change, drastic and fundamental change, they are faced with almost superhuman difficulties as regards understanding what such changes should be and how to bring them about.

We have to recognise what should be the first steps to take in order to break out of the muddled impasse in which the world is bogged down today. The need is for a rallying call for all who are young in spirit, ready for change, ready for endeavour and ready for co-operation.

What we are all waiting for is a new awakening to the fact that honesty, integrity and wisdom are a part of love; that if we love we cannot harm; we have to share; we have to work and plan together. If we love selflessly we know joy, and therefore our needs of all kinds become steadily less. Such needs as we will continue to experience must be answered only through love, creatively not collectively. Therefore we must have beautiful things created with love and with our hands, therefore works of art.

We must live in realisation of what we are—composite creatures, inherently part animal, part human, part angel; creatures in whom God, genius and the Devil (so-called) battle for supremacy. We are living in a world of illimitable mystery, wonder and potentiality, all of which finds anchorage within our tiny selves. For *we* are the creatures who can develop or spoil this beautiful planet and all life upon its surface, most of which life is still invisible to us. In our tiny hands is centred the power to upset, modify or improve the designs of mother nature, the power to build or destroy.

So far we have built with one hand and destroyed with the other. We create beauty and ugliness, order and squalor, with equal energy. We can be beastly or saintly, clever or stupid, effective or ineffective, whole or incomplete.

Yet in our essence we are a part of the Creator. We have, pulsing through all our being, our Creator's intent, energy, genius, and loving care. All this *is* flowing through us. But because we are made in the image of our Creator, with, in miniature, the same potential; because we are, in miniature, potential cosmic Creators, we have also to endure that enigma called 'free-will', and that other enigma called 'individuality'. We are burdened with the accumulations of aeons of wrongly used 'free-will'. Our deep descent into materialism has cut us off from the love and wisdom of our Creator, Who waits with patience for us to awaken to a true sense of values, to break out of our prison of fear, greed, and separativeness; to break out into the freedom of the 'second birth'; into the world of love, power, wisdom, responsibility and effectiveness.

We can all have beautiful and effective lives if we choose. We can change this planet into a Paradise compared with what she now is. For Mother Earth is a living being, destined to make inner intrinsic progress just as are we all, and depending upon us, who play the part of her mind-cells, to help her to do so, instead of endangering her very existence by our exploitation, destruction and poisoning of so much of her life.

The time is coming when a whole section of the community will rally round the banner of Love, which in its maturest expression is Integrity. For Love and Wisdom together produce Integrity—which is love made manifest in all earthly occupations. It is the password to creativity and fulfilment, and will produce Wisdom in Practice.

What, therefore, is Integrity, and how could it be so effective? A person of integrity is prepared to face truth in all its aspects, and to abide by what he sees. He assesses the effects and result of all his needs and actions, repudiating everything which exploits, divides, harms, or stultifies.

Christ taught us Integrity in many of its aspects. So did Buddha and other great Teachers. We have to learn to listen for the 'still small voice' in our hearts, which tells us instantly if a thing is right or wrong; whereas, the mind, contrary to the heart, will argue us back into our old selfish ruts.

Is it better to grab or to give? to hoard or to share? to love or to hate? to be healthy or diseased? joyful or resentful? energetic or lifeless? Is it better if our needs and habits do not necessitate suffering, drudgery, unpleasant work and ill health in those who supply our wants, or an unequal share of earth's gifts and no time to enjoy them?

If our needs do cause any of these states, then integrity requires that we change them!

For instance, would *we* prefer to create beautiful, interesting clothes by hand, stimulated by the pride of achievement, and with an outlet for our creative capacities—or—would we prefer to be cooped up in a noisy fume-filled factory, working at top speed like an automaton, without any variation or reward to look forward to? If we would prefer the former, then we must not inflict the latter way of life upon any human being by reason of the things we consider that we need. Instead, we must try increasingly to buy hand-made goods—or make them ourselves!

That is integrity.

Then let us think about coal. Would *we* prefer to work in the bowels of the earth, dirty and half blinded, our lungs in danger of deadly disease, not seeing sunshine or even daylight—a life of imprisonment, away from the joys of nature and our families?

If we would not like or approve of such a life, and if the thought of it shocks us—then we must try to do without coal, even little by little.

Integrity is as simple as that.

In fact the entire situation in industry and agriculture must come under our scrutiny. The ideal new-age relationships between employer, employee, union and customer must be envisaged with new eyes, in which complete sharing of ideas, benefits and enterprise can take place.

Next comes the question of diet. We have to face whether

flesh-eating is either a necessary or a natural custom? The answer, of course, scientifically and ethically, is *no*! Not only does it break the Commandment 'THOU SHALT NOT KILL', but it demonstrates the fact that one step downwards leads to fifty steps downwards, and ends in complete submergence—as we witness now, in a civilisation which is bent on self-annihilation in a dozen ways, and spoliation of all the elements of nature. Once embarked on this headlong descent into degeneracy, nothing is too low for man to demonstrate, from crime, vice, torturing and exploiting, vivisection, blood sports, warfare—the lot!

The flesh-eater is responsible for causing his fellow-man to be brutalised by appalling and disgusting work—and then causing more agony through the production of nauseous serums to cure the diseases caused by flesh-eating! It is a very vicious circle indeed, and one which integrity cannot allow.

Furthermore, one must remember one's responsibility to one's own body and mind, all of which is deeply affected by one's diet and the motives which allow it and direct it.

The recognition that man is essentially a fruitarian species, one who is at his best on a diet of raw fruits, nuts, greens and roots must be faced. Such a diet, approached little by little, would regenerate, rejuvenate and invigorate him, changing his outlook, his habits and his values. He would create a new type of horticulture which would regenerate and rejuvenate Mother Earth also, remodel world economy, and bring in at last a successful and happy civilisation.

These are a few of the changes which real integrity will bring about. We have dealt with them in our other books, but they must be emphasised here as the essential outcome of Wisdom in Practice.

Saved from chronic ill-health, apathy and mob pressure, men's minds would awaken and function in new ways. The spirit of responsibility and world guardianship would lead to the emergence of an inspired type of statesman and reformer instead of the usual type of politician.

Integrity produces thoroughness, wholeheartedness and joy in action. It can leave nothing out, and it brings the understanding of the interdependence of all life—and of all the kingdoms of nature, one with another. It brings dynamism, purposefulness, enterprise.

When enough people have reached such spiritual adulthood, they will find each other. Together they will form a spearhead, pioneering into the new age—a vanguard of vanguardians!

They will understand and demonstrate the words of Christ:

'Be ye wise as serpents and harmless as doves!'

23

Wisdom in Practice

In order to put wisdom into practice another new-age quality will come into play. This is known as the 'group spirit'. It is only attainable when self-centredness (and all its repercussions) has been melted away. Then people will stand together clear of separativeness, self-protection and fear. They will be concerned only for the good of the whole—the whole planet and all life upon her.

When finally this happy situation emerges, i.e. a world group of fellow-spirits bent on world regeneration, they will soon attain sufficient strength to persuade national governments to co-operate in fundamentally new ways of administration.

Let us enumerate some of them.

Firstly, the planet herself should be better understood. Instead of exploring the moon and neglecting their own planet, our world-guardians will seriously study forces and energies in existence around us, hitherto ignored.

We know that man has created many of the world's deserts. In so doing, he has also upset the wonderful natural water supply which is the blood-circulation of the planetary body. He has caused interruptions and alterations, causing Mother Earth in her discomfort to suffer from fevers and eruptions, such as volcanic calamities, earthquakes—cracks in her skin, upsets in her metabolism, and congestions in her etheric and electrical conditions (any human being can discover all this in miniature in his own body).

Amongst the many effects of these larger causes, the surface of the earth has acquired a mottled condition, so that places at small distances from each other exhibit great differences of quality. This is largely due to the fact that disturbances in the water formations often produce criss-cross channels or streams of water which have taken on unnatural directions. Crossing each other underground, they interfere with the beneficial play of the Cosmic Rays from outer space, whose work it is to produce quality, intelligence and development in all life.

When these Rays are deflected and thrown back, upwards in false directions, they produce tensions in many living creatures. This results in diseases such as cancer and tuberculosis gaining the upper hand. It also seriously inhibits the natural energy and awareness which is man's birthright.

Therefore we need all the wisdom we can attain in order to understand and rehabilitate conditions on the earth's surface which former generations, and perhaps our own, have disrupted and disoriented. In such ways must we learn to put first things first, and to leave the moon alone until we have done so! These first things are the very elements of life, the air, water, earth and sunshine, in their natural reaction upon each other. These relationships need to be so thoroughly understood that in time the planet will be prospected and mapped out and assessed so that an overall plan becomes feasible. This will ensure the right use of all land, its regeneration, and its suitability or otherwise for airfields, towns, orchards and factories. These findings should gradually become accepted and implemented by all nations, who would gladly pool their wisdom and inspiration in this cause. The waterways, and rail and road would also be planned to give the least waste of land or interruption of natural amenities. Reafforestation would be a major enterprise.

Wisdom in Practice would assure, therefore, the building of the new world civilisation from the ground upwards, and the inclusion of the Planetary well-being in its calculations. Thus a happier, healthier atmosphere would soon result for all.

The new group-spirit would bring about a far better understanding of human relationships. It will enable and encourage people to live together in Communities. This will become a major aspect of the new age. Signs of this development are already evident, for instance, in Israel. We might also study the results of Vinoba's reforms in India, where thousands of villages raised their standards of living through group co-operation, and self-help, followed by such villages co-operating with each other.

Amongst the rebellious youth of today, group living and group action is becoming more and more effective. Communities are coming quite naturally into existence, even if they are communities on the march! Concerted action among unregimented people is another new-age element, to be found the world over.

We can thus observe that decentralisation, freedom from self-centredness, normally results in the birth of the group spirit and of the quality of guardianship. This in its turn results in the upsurge of groups and Communities of many kinds. Some of these groups grow into organic Community Centres. Today it is not enough to form a 'society'. People now wish to live and demonstrate their beliefs and visions, to get free from the 'rat-race' and the chaos inherent in modern life, and to live together in fraternities which are evolving prototypes for the future. This, in fact, is a major aspect of Wisdom in Practice, out of which the new age civilisation will assuredly grow.

For if we consider which are the most pressing problems in the world today, we will be told that they are the problems of old age, loneliness, neglected children, delinquent youth, over-breeding, wrong nourishment, permissiveness, uncreative employment, and exploitation. And these are all the problems which can be happily solved in Community Centres.

Healthful living and enterprising occupations will do away with 'diseased old age'. Old people will become only *mature* people, with a fund of experience on which to draw; builders of new-age education, exerting guardianship over the little children of the Community. The very old and the very young will, together, constitute the heart of any Community, instead of, as now, becoming the problems of society.

In a Community everyone learns how to find his rightful expression and contribution. The value and privilege of work, even for its own sake, is eventually realised. Each Centre will foster its own particular expression of collective genius. Yet each Centre will give allegiance to certain major ethics and principles and laws of nature, which are necessary to the health of body, mind and soul, and exert repercussions on all life.

On these broad bases all can meet and co-operate, so that eventually there will be *Communities of Communities*! Each Community will recognise that it plays the part of a cell in the body of the new civilisation, and that, together, their concerted experience and guidance will build the foundations of the new world order, the coming world organisation—a World Government which at last expresses the goal :

'Government by the People for the People'—but it will be an enlightened People, inspired by world guardianship and love.

It is wonderful to observe, at the present time, that at last, after age-long trial and error, Community Centres are emerging which begin successfully to achieve many of the factors hitherto too difficult or too subtle to demonstrate. Your author has begun to study these emerging results at first hand.

There are so many aspects of successful living which must find their place in the new age, and which need to be studied. For instance, it should be borne in mind that the extraordinary new pressures which are being brought to bear upon the human psyche, in the field of radiation of many kinds, are having an overall effect upon the subtler sheaths of the human individuality. These sheaths function in and are built of matter of the four ethers. These are the medium for the five senses and are also used by their extended powers when developed.

These extensions of the five senses, which as we know are clairvoyance, clairaudience, psychometry, imagination and idealism, are isolated from the average person's control by the solidity of his own *etheric web*. This is thickened into tiny doors which shut him off from his extra sense perceptions (ESP) and insulate his higher energies also. These etheric doorkeepers protect the unevolved man from the danger of his inherent fires and faculties, which would be far too strong for him to support before he is sufficiently advanced.

Little by little, this web is worn away, both by the impinging radiations of outer scientific developments, and by the man's own inner advancement, through suffering, sacrifice and endeavour—all of which contribute to stepping up his vibrational rate. All over the world people are entering upon the next phase of development, wherein their five senses are extended and they become possessed of new faculties.

These phenomena are becoming so widespread that they are already accepted under the title of Extra Sense Perceptions (ESP). But as well as the extension of our well-known five senses, there will come also the extension of our sixth and seventh senses, giving us telepathy, intuition and prophetic powers, discrimination, healing, etc.

All these inherent capacities will be particularly apparent in certain types of advanced people who will be drawn to take part in Community Living. Therefore the educational centres which are to become the cornerstones in each Community must build up a type of education to meet the needs of ESP.

The new gifts will give people the power to communicate with and learn from the animal kingdom. Hence the absolute necessity for what I have called 'THE ABOLISHMENT OF ANIMAL SLAVERY', in which direction we are already seeing many signs.

Secondly, ESP will enable people to perceive and finally to communicate with the Deva kingdom and the kingdom of nature spirits. These, as you know, include beings from the highest angels to the tiniest fairies and elementals.

There is so much ahead, therefore, for the advancing human being to experience that it staggers the imagination. His ideas about birth and death, mind and sex, will undergo radical changes. The whole difficult problem of sex will be enlightened out of all recognition. Amazing future potentialities will be unveiled when the true secrets of sex and creativity are gifted to humanity, because it has earned the right and the power to know and to use them.

Most of what we have said in this chapter has been touched upon in our former books, and will be enlarged upon in our subsequent ones. Meanwhile your author would welcome any comments, suggestions and information relevant to these subjects, and especially in regard to existing Community Centres.

It has needed generations of faithful torchbearers to bring us to the point in the history of humanity when so many progressive changes are faced as now—not by a few leaders only, but by multitudes of the people everywhere. It is most important that we are not deceived and engrossed by the other and more violent side of the picture—the horrors, cruelty and treachery attendant on the modern forces of aggression. Let us always remember that the stimulation which is at work today must necessarily inflame and draw forth the evil while it arouses the good. Let us always remember that this period is like no other in history, that it *is* a world-wide cataclysm, crisis and upheaval, that it constitutes the birth throes of a new civilisation and a new awareness and set of values for humanity—and that these will be of a quality so stupendous in their ultimate developments that it would be difficult successfully to describe them here. That attempt has already been made in a former book,* which contained much that sounded far-fetched then but which is already being quietly envisaged and supported by the people today.

Soon the love of the human heart which is so aching to be set free will be given a measure of release and fulfilment in the new principles which are being set up as the foundations of the international economics of the future—those of giving and sharing.

There is a truth new to us which must soon be realised. This is that the only wealth existing in the world is the human being, with his work, his needs, his life-urge and his creative intellect. Money is actually false wealth as it is used today. The present idea that goods should represent wealth, although much less false, is still incorrect. The most precious thing in existence on this earth is certainly the human soul and individuality, the Son of God, and that is what rightly should be considered to be the wealth of the world. It will soon be seen that the riches and the potential of a country must be assessed not by money, not by goods, not even by human labour—but by the quality of the soul and life-motive of the people who produce all this. Such is the true wealth 'which neither moth nor rust doth corrupt'. The accruing interest of a country's riches should be the measure of her success in developing the spiritual and creative potential of her people; the building-up of a splendid life-motive which should ensure the quality of the generations to come. The national resources should be invested in human beings instead of in armaments or business concerns. Until every human being is entitled from birth to receive the best that modern civilisation can offer him in the necessities of living, and in spiritual and psychological training; until care is ensured that he is not only fully trained in useful service but inspired by the life-motive for that service—until all this essential work is fully assured, the resources of a nation should be spent in no other way. It should be felt that when a country invests money abroad whilst there are slums and unemployment at home, she stands convicted of an immoral and confused treatment of the simplest elements of economics and of her first responsibility.

* See *The Fifth Dimension,* Rider & Co.

If this were to come about, self-development and the development of the future generations would become the absorbing occupation of mankind. The potentialities of the human being would come to be realised and appreciated as never before, whilst material possessions as such would decline in importance.

When the time comes for the new organisation of the world which will provide every man with his fair share of mental and physical needs, mental conditions will change out of all recognition.

Fear, drudgery, despondency, ill-health, malnutrition and the other results of a 'capitalist' civilisation will disappear. What kind of a new humanity will be set free?

Unthinking people sometimes say that if man were not forced to work he would be lazy.

On the contrary, the natural state of human beings is joyous, energetic and creative. Conditions of living have sapped at least eight-tenths of their natural energy, and inhibitions have vitiated the rest of it.

What will happen to people when their minds are set free from the burden of perpetual worry and drudgery for the bare needs of daily life—often, even so, a losing battle? The freed mind will begin to delight in the wonders of the universe and in its own potentialities. Romance will come into the world in place of the humdrum. Romance, which is the appreciation of the mystery and promise which lies behind every outward form and activity. The Romance of spiritual achievement is the greatest romance of all. Once attained, it can be reflected into every simple daily task bringing to it a new interpretation and a new joy.

This *is* the kind of world which we are fighting for now, because it is the *only alternative* to present conditions. Humanity has achieved the privilege of sharing in the Crucifixion of Christ at last, in preparation for sharing in His resurrection and the new life. It is the great chance for all of us. Let us not 'sleep in the Garden of Gethsemane' as the disciples did, or we shall be found wanting, and desert our convictions and our own souls in the time of testing. But rather let us participate in this 'cold war of Armageddon', in its sufferings, its lessons and its opportunities, with everything that is in us. He who refuses to share in the Crucifixion cannot share in the glories which come after it.

Before we close this book let us note down in a few words the conclusions to which, with as much logic as we could apply, we have finally come :

Every human being has an intimate part in and an influence on the life of the whole planet, and a share in responsibility for present conditions.

Every human being is a potential source of unpredictable power which can be tapped in an emergency or under unusual stimulation.

This power is usually split up and divided against itself by destructive thought-processes which we call inhibitions.

It can be co-ordinated by developing a single wholehearted life-motive based upon spiritual laws.

These conditions apply both to the individual and to the race when considered as a whole.

The life-motive so badly needed is the will to co-operate with the Divine Purpose and Plan of Evolution, and to give warm response to all the bounty received.

All races possess the jewels of spiritual lore and teaching to this end.

Christ brought these teachings to full power by crowning them with the simple Doctrine of Love.

When humanity is ready to build civilisation on the foundations of Love for God and Man, a Golden Age will begin. That time is now approaching, but it can come about only through the co-operation of each one of us.

When a sufficient number of men and women are living wholeheartedly, spiritually, and constructively, they will produce a tide of power that will swing the whole world into the new way of life—with new awareness, new understanding, new ideals and new health.

Those of us who are determined to strive for this goal can do certain things.

We can apply self-analysis, strip ourselves of mental débris, and put on the armour of our true life-motive.

We can repeat this process at regular intervals, in order to keep ourselves always in fighting trim.

We can begin to keep the greatest Commandment—to practise the art of Love-Wisdom, the love and understanding of God, ourselves, our neighbours, and all that is.

We can offer all we have to give in practical thought to our community, our country and our world.

We can meditate in the silence each day, in order to draw guidance and inspiration from the realms of soul and spirit.

We can link up in strength and comradeship with the many who are thinking and striving as we do. If my readers will communicate with me I will gladly help with this linking.

We can link up in understanding and love with all those who do *not* think as we do !

We can keep our courage high, our hearts serene, our vision clear, and our lives and those around us irradiated by that joy which is the hall-mark of the human being who has re-turned to God.